What Dying Taught Me about Living

Scott Drummond with Sandy Ponton

ISBN 979-8-88851-535-8 (Paperback)
ISBN 979-8-88851-537-2 (Hardcover)
ISBN 979-8-88851-536-5 (Digital)

Covenant Books
11661 Hwy 707
Murrells Inlet, SC 29576
www.covenantbooks.com

To my wife, Connie, without whose patience, love, understanding, and sacrifice this would not have been possible.
I am an ordinary man married to an
extraordinary, beautiful woman.

SCOTT WITH WIFE, CONNIE

Foreword

The first time I heard anything about near-death experiences (NDEs) was when I saw Raymond Moody Jr., MD, PhD's first book *Life After Life* at a bookstore in 1982. I read it and found it familiar even though I had never heard of it before, or of people having NDEs. A few years later when I became an attorney and radio talk-show host, I tracked down Raymond Moody and interviewed him for three hours on my radio show. Soon after I interviewed George Ritchie, MD, after reading his book *Return from Tomorrow*. One of the more compelling interviews I experienced was interviewing Melvin Morse, MD, together with his young patient "Katie" who had drowned in a swimming pool and been in a coma for three days, only to wake and describe seeing the heavenly Father and Jesus in heaven. Although none of the NDEs I had heard seemed contrived, I found it especially compelling that a little girl would have such a detailed experience she could never have made up.

Dozens of interviews followed, one with two women from the Seattle area, Pat Higby and Betty Eadie, which led to the writing of *Embraced by the Light*. After cofounding Utah IANDS in 1990 with Lynn Johnson, PhD, and NDE author Arvin Gibson, who went on to the next life, about which he had eagerly studied with his beloved wife, Carol, and so eloquently wrote about in five books over more than a decade. Most but not all will have heard of the International Association for Near-Death Studies (IANDS) Inc. with headquarters in North Carolina, after which Utah IANDS was patterned.

To date, I have personally interviewed over six hundred people who have had NDE. Few have been more compelling than the NDE of Scott Drummond described in detail in this book. I heard about Scott's NDE on YouTube from a friend, Paul Norat, who thought it had an extraordinary quality and down-to-earth sincerity. I tracked down Scott, heard his experience firsthand, and invited him to speak to an audience at Utah IANDS. As Scott began to share his experience, his humility, sincerity, and desire to reassure people during troubled times were apparent. This was in October 2021. In some places, COVID lockdowns were still damaging and destroying businesses. Many people were still wearing masks, and children in many areas were still unable to attend school in person. In this context, Scott Drummond's NDE was even more wonderful, providing comfort in an anxiety-filled world. Many, many others have had the same reaction. Scott's NDE on YouTube has at the time of this writing had over twenty-one million views. This is an extraordinary number. Now and indefinitely into the future, those who read Scott Drummond's NDE in this book will find peace, and their faith in a life beyond this one will be kindled or strengthened. Scott has now spoken in many places throughout the United States and elsewhere. He spoke at the 2022 International IANDS Conference and was very well received. People were changed and moved.

Throughout history, every person, at some point in their life, is faced with the implications of death, for themself or another who has died, had an accident or an illness, or had otherwise glimpsed or contemplated the next life. Thus, it should be no surprise to anyone that Scott's NDE described in this book has been popular and will continue to be.

Although critics and skeptics will continue to doubt NDEs are real, Scott's account, following the many thousands which have preceded it, and the many others which will no doubt come after it, stands as a unique and exceptionally strong declaration and testimony that there is a life beyond this one. It would be hard for me to imagine how, after hearing Scott's humble and sincere words, one could doubt he actually experienced what he describes in this book.

For my own part, I am content that whatever anyone else chooses to believe, I am convinced Scott Drummond experienced exactly what he describes hereafter in the pages of this book. I have heard him relate his experience several times now. The descriptions of what he saw and experienced do not change. Perhaps the greatest indicia of the authenticity of an NDE is how it has impacted and changed the life of the person who experienced it and how it has changed the lives of those who have heard it. On both counts, I am persuaded Scott's NDE is true. Scott's life and millions of lives have been changed by his NDE. Scott Drummond has a deep sense of peace, a depth of kindness, genuine empathy and understanding, and true love and concern for all people. This makes him remarkable in a world filled which has too much anger, pessimism, and criticism.

It is therefore a genuine honor and great pleasure to introduce you to my friend Scott Drummond and his remarkable near-death experience. I am confident that through this book, you will have some sense of his kind heart and loving personality.

Martin Tanner, JD
IANDS Vice President
Co-Founder and Chair, Utah IANDS
October 26, 2022

Preface

It is impossible to know the impact our actions and even just our existence can have on the lives of those around us. The film *It's a Wonderful Life* will always remain a classic, and the message it teaches always rings true. Every one of us is important. We all have meaning, and if you were suddenly out of the picture, the world would be worse off for it.

I truly believe this. Most of us will not share a story from our lives and have it reach millions like Scott Drummond, but we are all in this together, and we all impact many more people in our lives than we realize.

With that being said, the impact that has come from two simple neighbors getting together to share a story that we felt we needed to share is still mind-boggling. Only two years since the video went up, and it has over twenty-one million views.

The impact of this story can be seen by looking over the comments. There are far too many wonderful comments to share here, but many of these comments have blessed my life, just as Scott's experience has.

Below is a very small excerpt of some of the comments. First, there have been countless people explaining that Scott's story has helped them overcome a fear of death:

- "Thanks for sharing your story! One of my children has extreme anxiety about death, and your story has helped immensely. I'm sure I am not the only one who really needed your story. Thanks again!"

Thousands of comments on how the story increased their faith:

- "I needed this. I have been struggling with a war inside myself with my faith."
- "*Wow*. My faith has strengthened. Bless you."
- "Thank you for sharing. I have been struggling with my faith for the last year."
- "Your story is a blessing to me, personally. You've enhanced my faith with your story. God bless you and your family. Thank you."
- "Amazing human being, thank you for sharing your story. This restores my faith."
- "I've struggled with faith for many years due to an abusive earthly father. Your story changed my mind. Thank you!"
- "There's got to be something out there after death. This guy has just reinforced that belief in me. Thank you."

Even thousands more of people find comfort when they have lost a loved one:

- "I would stay awake every night crying about death and how I would never see my mum again and my sister my friend, but you've given me hope. Thank you."
- "I lost my parents nine months apart in 2014. Sometimes the grief is just overwhelming. This video gave me a lot of comfort. Thank you for sharing your story."
- "Thank you. I lost my son a year ago, and I can't get past the pain of losing my child. This has helped me."
- "Lost my dad a week ago, and I needed to hear this to be able to go on with my life. But hearing this and knowing my dad is at peace made me feel better inside."
- "Thank you for sharing your story with us. I lost my daughter recently in a motorcycle accident three thousand miles away from home. The pain and sadness I feel thinking she suffered make me cry because she was our world. I'm grateful for your story. It brings me peace."

- "I needed this today so bad. My dad died two weeks ago, and I have been struggling terribly. So thank you."
- "My dad passed away six weeks ago, and this has brought me so much peace to know my dad is safe and well."

So many other thousands of comments thanking Scott for his message and for what it brought to their lives:

- "Incredible, just incredible. Tears are rolling. Thank you so much for sharing, and glory to God for revealing your purpose to you here on earth."
- "Did anyone else just get some clarity hearing this? This made me happy and a bit shaken to think about prioritizing my life."

Finally, a comment about Scott, and one that I deeply agree with. He is a simple and humble man that would have never wanted or asked for this kind of exposure. I feel, in part, that is why his story has appealed to so many people. You can just sense that he is a good man without some ulterior motive. I thank God for being a part of bringing Scott's story to the world.

- "What a beautiful story by a man with a beautiful soul."

Wesly Lapioli
Host of Prioritize Your Life

Testimonials

As a fellow near-death experiencer, NDE educator, and therapist, discovering Scott's YouTube video describing his NDE was a blessing to my life and the lives of millions around the world. Thankfully, after forty years of public silence about his spiritual experience, Scott decided to share this story with a filmmaker friend who politely coaxed him to be filmed so that he could share his NDE publicly to help those who were suffering from losses during the COVID-19 pandemic. The video went viral, making Scott an international sensation with over twenty million views. His captivating life and death experience and his message of hope and joy and his no longer fearing death have touched our hearts completely.

—Lilia Samoilo
Four-time NDEr, NDE Educator, Advocate,
and Consultant for Combat Veterans

Scott first publicly talked about his NDE at the 2022 IANDS Conference, and I was so awed and touched by his emotional recall of the event, laced with such detail, after holding it inside his heart and not disclosing it to anyone for over forty years. Scott's NDE account should sway any skeptic... *NDEs are real* and can happen to anyone. We who have experienced them never asked for the NDE to happen. Most of us didn't even know they were possible, but our lives and our life path are awesomely enhanced by our NDE, and we feel that it's important to find a way to share how we've learned, grown, and gained from the NDE we were gifted. Warm thanks to Scott for opening up about his beautiful NDE…and passing its radiant gifts out to humanity.

—Barbara Bartolome
Two-time NDEr and Founder/Group
Leader of IANDS Santa Barbara

Scott and his amazing experience has had a profound effect on me. It has helped me feel more grateful for my own life and the lessons and gifts that God has given me. Scott is truly an inspiration!

—Vinney Todd Tolman
Author

Since I was a young child, I remember my father telling me how he was in a horrible ski accident and how he was pronounced dead and brought back to life. He was given the gift of coming back and had a second chance at life. I never heard the story of his near-death experience entirely until last year. As a child, I was in awe of his gift, but hearing it as an adult, I've taken so much from it.

He felt as if it's the right time to share, to bring peace and hope to others—especially now with everything going on in the world from COVID to politics that are dividing us rather than bringing one another closer. I am proud of his bravery! What a courageous thing for him to be able to open up and share an experience that is so close to his heart and sacred.

There is so much peace that comes with his story. Now as an adult, I've realized that there is so much more to life. I have now wanted to focus more on my purpose. It connects me with the love within so I can make my mark on the world. As Christ says, out of all things, love is what matters most. I have to remember the important things. And through my father's story, I have felt like it's been a huge blessing for me, knowing I too have a second chance. I am re-prioritizing my life, changing things that are in my hands, and sharing my testimony with others. I am focusing more on my happiness and preparing myself more every day so I can come unto Christ knowing I did my best. It brings great comfort knowing the process and having faith in knowing this life is just a glimpse of what eternity will be like. I have to continue with faith, putting in the work to be worthy of my heavenly Father. I cannot wait to be with Him again, having my family and daughter for all eternity.

I have watched my father receive many, many calls and messages from people all over the world. He has touched so many lives! People are in awe of his near-death experience. It brings peace and hope to those who do need it most—those who do not have the knowledge or belief that God is real, that life after death is beautiful, pure, and sacred.

Each of these messages has been heartfelt. I love that it has touched so many lives. It's so comforting! I have gotten a glimpse of his responses, and it's been truly amazing how many people it has touched and brought such joy! It has affected so many people in such a positive way that it's overwhelming with such warmth in my heart, and especially his! I truly believe the world needs to hear those messages. I know he was prompted by our Savior, Jesus Christ, to finally open up, even though it's such a sacred, personal experience. The world needed to hear it, mostly right now where there is so much darkness that any light shown down is bringing us closer to God.

I can feel and relate to others who may feel that there is no more hope, that life is just too hard. So I pray for our Savior's return. I cannot wait to come unto Christ and fall into His arms. I can feel His love all around me. I have to remember that He loves us all! One of my favorite quotes is by Glen Fitzjerrell: "Jesus told the story of the Prodigal Son to make a simple point: never mind what you've done. Just come home."

Through my father's near-death experience, I too have been given a second chance. I am forever grateful.

—Chelsea Drummond,
Daughter of Scott Drummond

I strongly believe that what my grandfather saw during his near-death experience is the truth. They say that your life flashes before your eyes when you die. Isn't what my grandpa describes just that? Only bringing forth more clarity on the subject. Rather than a flurry of moments, it is like reliving your life all over again; only you're able to see all that you did from a different emotional perspective. It lets you see what you have done and how you have spent your life. It certainly makes more sense to me than flashes of time.

That isn't the only thing my grandpa told of, however. He also spoke deeply of the love that surrounded him when he passed to the other side. When I look at nature here on earth, I am taken in by the majesty and the glory that we have here. It's a taste of what I'm sure my grandpa felt. It's love because it's been created by a loving God. That love is unconditional, and it is eternal. What a beautiful thing to be able to feel such love after your spirit leaves your body, to feel such peace and companionship with someone even after your life on earth is over, and to know that true conversation is not through the spoken word but through thoughts and compassion for others.

The transfer between life and death is perhaps more peaceful than we give it credit for. Not to mention what's after has a great purpose for our souls, whatever that may be. Though it was not my grandpa's time to leave us quite yet, as he returned to his body, he was given a second chance to improve himself. Though I did not know him at the time of his near-death experience, I know him now. He is a kind, honest man who shows love and compassion to all those he meets. He shows that unconditional love I'm sure he felt. He has this astonishing gift to be able to make plants flourish in ways no one else can. He is a good, wise, and kind man that went through something so personal and sacred to him, yet when the time came for him to share it, he did. Why? Because it's all about being able to speak to at least one person, to help at least one person. For the worth of one person is far greater than any of us will be able to fully comprehend.

—Zoie Miller,
Granddaughter of Scott Drummond

Chapter 1

You know those days when you feel like the universe is out to get you? June 13, 1991, was just such a day for me. If I'd known that statistics, and the hand of fate, were stacked against me on that particular day, I might've stayed home. The event was so spectacular; it left a literal black mark on the ground that remained years later, and all from an innocuous round of golf.

Sports have always been a big deal to me. More than just a pastime or hobby, throughout my life, sports have been my refuge. You could even say they saved my life. That being said, a spontaneous round of golf with a friend is something I'm always up for. On that fateful day in 1991, I called up a good friend of mine, Frank Purvis, and asked if he'd like to play a round.

Back in the day, Frank was a lineman for the University of Florida. If you don't have the foggiest idea what a lineman is, they're usually the biggest, heaviest, baddest guys on a football field. I wasn't a football player in college, but I played baseball for Brigham Young University. Frank and I were a bit out of our college ball days, but we still loved sports.

Playing golf with Frank wasn't out of the ordinary for me, but on this day in particular, I knew I shouldn't have called him. My wife was at a sewing conference with her mother and sister—an outing they'd planned for months—and I had promised to watch our kids while she was gone. As sports are for me, sewing is for my wife. That knowledge should have been enough to keep me home, but I only wanted to play a quick round, and I felt confident Frank and I could get back home before she returned from her conference. At least, that's what I told myself.

Frank probably wasn't in the best position to go with me either. His wife had just given birth to their baby the day before. Not exactly the best time to lure my friend away from his wife with a *quick* round of golf. But we used that as our justification: the celebration of Frank's new arrival.

For those of you who know little about the sport, a round of golf is anything but quick. It isn't a fast-paced game of two-on-two basketball; it's a sedate and methodical sport that can take hours. In fact, the average golf course roughly amounts to a five-mile walk.

Despite the compelling reasons to put off our outing for a better day, Frank and I set out for the Cascade Golf Course. Being June, the weather was nice but unpredictable. By the time we reached the third hole, we could see a storm far off in the distance. The golf course was at the foothills of the Wasatch Mountains, and the dark, heavy clouds of the storm were barely creeping across Utah Lake that lay settled in the basin of the valley. Not easily deterred, Frank and I felt confident we had plenty of time to finish the round before the storm arrived.

We were finishing the eighth hole, and I was just walking off the green after a putt I'll never forget. It was one of those magical moments when the painstaking finesse of putting came together perfectly, and I nailed it. It was the putt of a lifetime! The next thing I knew, something hit me with the force of a battering ram and knocked me a good fifteen feet off the green. When my head cleared and I got my bearings, everything I saw was in a whiteout, and the ground was full of electricity. The only thing I could hear was the horrifying sounds of agonizing pain coming from my friend, Frank.

Come to find out, being struck by lightning doesn't feel good.

According to the Centers for Disease Control and Prevention (CDC), the odds of being struck by lightning are one in a million, and almost everyone survives.

However.

Being a guy makes you four times more likely to be struck; I'm a guy. The month of June is only beaten by July as the month most likely to be struck in; it was June. Nationally, the Rocky Mountain Range—which the Wasatch Mountains are a part of—ranks among the highest for lightning deaths and injuries during the summer months; it was summer in the Rockies. And outdoor recreation is the culprit for nearly two-thirds of lightning strike deaths; we were golfing.

To sum up, Frank and I were very lucky to be alive, especially when my wife later relayed the prophetic words she had uttered to our son when she called our home for a quick check on the kids. She had asked them how they were doing with their chores and quickly discovered that I wasn't watching them as I'd promised. I had gone golfing instead. Being the wise woman she is, she had said, "Oh my gosh! He's going to be hit by lightning."

After the strike, all I could think about was getting Frank immediate medical care. He ended up being in the hospital for a while and underwent multiple surgeries throughout the following years. The lightning had struck Frank in the head and exited out his back causing serious injury.

As for me, after seeing into Frank's medical care, I just went home. It didn't occur to me to get myself checked out. Frank was the one in unbelievable pain. My discomfort was nothing compared to what he endured. The lightning had hit my head. It struck the Squatchee—the fabric-covered button—on the top of my baseball hat, went down through my body, and out through my feet. My baseball hat was shredded, my shirt had a black streak down the back, my feet were hot and sensitive, and I peed electricity for a week. It was nothing compared to what Frank had to go through.

It wasn't until much later that I discovered the magnitude of what had happened—the damage it had done to both of us.

Years later when I reminisced with Frank, his version was much more detailed. He recounted things I couldn't have known. He'd even written it all down in his journal. The following is his written account concerning the events of that day in his own words.

*****

14 December 2021

When Scott called and asked me for my perspective on the accident that had happened over thirty years ago, I was glad that I had a few notes written down about it.

My second son, Kyle, was born on 12 June 1991. The next day, June 13th, Scott called and asked if I wanted to go golfing to celebrate, and I was a little hesitant at first. But we knew we had plenty of time. So we went to Cascade Golf in Orem, Utah. We were golfing just fine. We noticed it was getting a little cloudy, but we felt we could finish before it would start raining or be too windy on the course.

We made our rounds to the eighth hole and had just finished up with putting and getting ready to walk to the ninth-hole tee box. As we began to walk to the ninth-hole tee box, I started feeling the hair on my arms tingle and heard a rattling noise that seemed to get faster as we kept walking. Then in an instant, everything changed. I saw a light so bright it made everything around me look brilliantly white, a white that was beyond my description. I looked at my arm, and it was as if I was in slow motion, and then a pain struck that I had never felt before. My head felt like it was beating out of my skull. I looked all around me, and everything was bright white. I saw Scott grab at his head, then I saw his head explode. I thought, *Oh my gosh. He's dead.* Then everything seemed to be a blur. We had been hit by lightning, and I didn't know what to do. I remember falling to the ground thinking Scott was dead, and so was I. I don't know to this day how I got up off the ground. I can't tell you how fast it happened or how much time had elapsed. Time had no concept to me.

In this moment, I felt at peace and did not have any worries. I saw my dad (who passed away in 1974) when I was walking—I don't know where I was walking; I was just walking around. He told me that I had to leave and that I had three sons to raise. He smiled and then disappeared. When I woke up, I saw Scott laying on the ground. I knew he must be dead, so I looked and saw it was his baseball cap that had exploded. He seemed to be moving.

I laughed a little. He looked like someone had used him as a candle. Some smoke was coming out of the top of his head. Up to this time, I felt like everything was in slow motion, super slow motion. The colors were coming back, and yet I didn't know where I was or how I ever got back, and it was all just a blur.

In the time I was there, I saw things and was told they were sacred and not to make light of it—so I don't. I was so happy that I was alive and learned from this just to keep moving forward and love my wife and family. So in a way, I learned what was important to me and be thankful for all I have been given!

I had back surgery in July of that year as a direct result of the lightning strike. The strike entered my head and exited out my back, causing the L4 and L5 to explode. The doctor had to wait for the swelling to go down before he could operate. I've had two subsequent surgeries on my back as a result of the lightning strike.

And yes, I had a third son six years later. We almost gave up trying to have more children, but miraculously we were able to have one more son to complete our family.

So Scott and I, that day in my mind, got a little glimpse of what waits for us, and I am just happy that I was able to heal.

Side note: I had to give up golf after the surgeries. But what I gave up, I gained so very much more.

I attest that on 13 June 1991, this really happened, and I have the scars and the love to know that it is true.

Thank you,
Marion Frank Purvis
14 December 2021

*****

Looking back on that day, the event was a merciful reminder for me. A heavenly kick in the pants, if you will. There were things I had been careless with, and now was the time to pay better attention.

Frank went back to the same spot on the golf course a while after the lightning strike. There on the ground was a black mark, left to remind us of another chance at life. For me, it was more than a second chance; it was a third. It was a reminder of a previous experience too beautiful for words, a gift from God that I'd left on a dusty shelf and neglected.

It was a loving reminder of the day I died.

Chapter 2

At the heart of the Wasatch Mountain Range lies the Park City Mountain Resort. At the time of this writing, Park City was the largest ski resort in the United States, and one of its busiest times of year is the New Year holiday. Skiers at every skill level and from around the world flock to what is dubbed "the Greatest Snow on Earth." For most skiers, their experience at the resort includes features like bunny hills, moguls, black diamond runs, and chairlifts.

Unfortunately for me, on January 1, 1981, my experience inexplicably led to my untimely death.

In 1981, I was twenty-eight years old, and snow skiing was a big part of my wintertime regimen. December, January, and February were the months to cram in as much time skiing as possible, and being out on the slopes on the New Year break was a particular tradition for my friend and me. Because the occasion was normal for us, the crush of holiday skiers and long lines for the chairlift weren't anything out of the ordinary. The air was crisp, the skies were partly cloudy, and the snow was excellent. That's all we cared about.

While shooshing along in the congested serpentine line for the chairlift, attention suddenly drew to a novice skier careening down the ski run. Arms flailing, poles windmilling, the woman was in obvious distress and completely out of control, not to mention making a beeline for the skiers waiting for the lift. She was powerless to do anything but yell, "Look out!" As for the skiers packed in the line, there wasn't much wiggle room available for them to get out of the way. Like a kamikaze, the poor woman plowed straight into the crowd. Her unintentional and unsuspecting target? Me.

Like pins at the end of a bowling lane, a good handful of us ended up knocked over, our gear scattered across the snow. Instead of worrying about myself, my first concern was for the woman who'd crashed into me. A couple of guys and I got the woman to her feet and made sure she was okay. She was in her early thirties and dressed to the nines in expensive designer ski gear. She even wore a tan furry hat that looked like a stacked wedding cake. Thankfully, other than a healthy dose of embarrassment, she seemed unharmed and eager to get on her way.

Park City's summit elevation comes in at a whopping 10,026 feet. That kind of altitude contributes to its claim of exceptional snow, but on a partly cloudy day in January, it makes for extremely low temperatures. Often, even top-of-the-line ski apparel can't compete with the frigid air—especially in the extremities. Glowing-red noses and cheeks and numbed faces, feet, and hands are common. For most, it's enough to relegate them to the resort's lodge with a good book and a steaming cup of cocoa by a fire. For a twenty-eight-year-old guy who relished any opportunity to be out on the ski runs, the cold was little more than a minor annoyance.

My friend and I skied until closing, as was our habit, eking out as much fun as possible. Buzzing from a great day on the mountain, we headed to the car and began shedding our outer layers.

One of the more enjoyable parts of taking off ski gear after a long day is releasing the bindings on ski boots. In case you don't know much about ski gear, bindings cinch the ski boot tight around the lower leg, ankle, and foot, so when the clunky boot clips into the ski, it becomes a sturdy extension of the leg. At the end of a long day, finally releasing those tight bindings spells sweet relief.

In 1981, they chiefly made ski boot bindings out of metal. Often they would freeze shut, making releasing them a chore. To open mine, I knew I would need a good grip to wrench the binding open, so I yanked the glove off my right hand to get a firm hold. It wasn't until I pulled the ski glove from my hand that I suddenly realized the accident in the lift line had done more damage than I thought. Holding my hand up in front of my face, I saw that all my fingers stood up like they should, except for my thumb, which now hung limply down to my wrist, attached only by the skin.

How could I have not known my hand was in such bad shape? It didn't take long to realize how easy it was to have ignored my injury. There were two factors, really. One, my padded ski gloves formed into a shape that made grasping ski poles easier. It held my fingers and hand in a natural position and kept my thumb from flopping down. But why didn't I feel the pain? That was the second factor. That same frigid weather—the kind that chased less fanatical skiers into the lodge—had kept my nose, toes, and hands/thumb at a numbing temperature. It was why I hadn't felt the pain.

Thankfully, the friend I was skiing with was an EMT (emergency medical technician) at the time. His skills really came in handy as we examined my hand. Having injured my thumb in sports before, though, I knew this injury was more than a simple dislocation. From the gruesome angle of my thumb, it was clear I'd need more help than a Band-Aid or an attempt at popping it back into place. Soon we decided it would be best to call my wife and tell her what happened. She could make the necessary phone calls and arrangements at the hospital while we made the long drive down the mountain.

Not long after we started down the road, the pain from my injury became uncomfortable. While at the resort, my hand had been cold and numb. Now with the heater in the car warming the air and my hands, the pain became increasingly severe.

The hour-long drive to Utah Valley Hospital seemed interminable. I knew the sooner we got there, the sooner I'd finally get relief from the terrible pain, but never in a million years could I have known we were speeding toward my premature death.

Chapter 3

My wife, Connie, was waiting nervously for me when we pulled up to the hospital's emergency room entrance. She'd made all the arrangements, and the orthopedic surgeon was expecting me. He was a tall man with blond-brown hair and glasses who was probably somewhere in his forties. In no time at all, the staff whisked me into the back while Connie waited out in the hall.

As they prepped me for surgery, the doctor mentioned how lucky I was to have made it to the hospital when I did. To him, it meant that he could likely save my thumb. While this was a relief, he followed up the statement by informing me that the anesthesiologist had been unexpectedly called away and wouldn't be able to help with the procedure. However, he assured me he didn't see this as too much of a problem because he knew of another solution that would allow him to perform the surgery without knocking me out. The technique was called a Bier block.

A Bier block, to put it as simply as I can, is a local anesthetic often used when a relatively simple surgery is required for an extremity. With a hand injury, the procedure starts with an IV and a pneumatic (air) tourniquet wrapped around the upper arm. Before inflating the cuff, the nurse elevates the arm so the blood will rush out of it. Then the tourniquet inflates to cut off circulation to the arm and hand. When no pulse is present in the arm, the nurse lowers it and injects anesthesia into the IV. As soon as the anesthesia reaches the right level, the surgery can begin.

When the doctor mentioned his intent to use a Bier block, the nurse let him know she'd never performed the procedure. I remember she had brown hair and was pretty young—I'd say, in her mid-twenties. Despite her misgivings and lack of training, the doctor expressed his confidence that he could talk her through it. Appeased, the nurse agreed to move forward with the unfamiliar technique.

At first, everything was going fine. The process seemed simple enough. They put a sheet up between me and the doctor that blocked my view of what was happening with my hand. As the doctor worked, I could talk to the nurse and let her know when the pain in my arm was getting uncomfortable. She acted professionally, had a good bedside manner, and was always sweet and kind. She would adjust some valves here and there and that would help me feel better.

Unfortunately, in 1981, machines didn't control the pressure levels in pneumatic tourniquets. The nurse had to do it manually, and it was a delicate sort of dance to keep things flowing right. In our day, most pneumatic tourniquets inflate and deflate based on what they're programmed to do. In 1981, if the nurse didn't keep the tourniquets and flow of anesthesia coordinated just right, things could go badly. As it did in my case. While the nurse tried to keep the pressure and anesthesia at precise levels, tragedy struck. Somewhere in that delicate dance, an accident occurred. One wrong turn of a valve, and I felt the anesthesia, which was meant to keep my arm and hand numb, suddenly race up my arm, across my chest, and into my heart.

The effect killed me instantly.

Chapter 4

The next thing I knew, I was standing in the air above my body. Every ounce of pain was suddenly, inexplicably gone. I felt no fear, no anxiety, no stress. Instead all I felt was tremendous peace. Imagine it, to feel complete and total peace? I'd felt nothing remotely like it in my life. More than being simply happy or calm in the way we experience it in mortality, it was a pure and utter otherworldly peace.

Below me, I saw the doctor working calmly and diligently. The poor nurse had a very different response. Distressed and panicked, she abruptly fled the room. I could hear the fear in her voice when she lamented loudly and clearly that she'd killed me. Soon the room flooded with medical staff desperately trying to revive me.

It's an odd thing to observe your own body laid out on a table, people rushing about to bring you back to life, and the raucous sounds of alarms and urgent orders. Sometimes people who contact me wonder why the doctor continued to work on my hand even though I had flatlined. It wasn't until years after the incident that I found out doctors are required to finish their work, whether the patient lives or dies. I never saw that nurse again though. I still wish I had, so I could tell her it wasn't her fault and that I didn't blame her.

Another key moment after I left my body came when I realized I wasn't alone where I stood in the air. There was someone else standing near me—another unseen person observing the melee below. I couldn't see this person, as he was in the blind spot behind and to the right of me. I knew the person was male because I could hear his voice. I don't know who he was, but I'll recognize that voice if I ever hear it again. His voice was calming and comforting, but it surprised me to find I couldn't hear it audibly. The frenzied sounds of the operating room I could hear with my ears, but this *guide's* voice came to my mind. Interestingly enough, I found I could answer and converse with him in the same way, and I somehow knew he was there to help me.

We watched the doctor work and the ministrations of the people who were there trying to revive me. With my ears, I could hear them talking and could see the commotion going on in the room. The doctor was diligent in finishing his surgery. It really impressed me and the person standing near me expressed that he was happy with what was going on. We watched him cut me open and lay out my thumb. He made an incision down my forearm, removed a tendon, and wrapped it around my thumb. We watched him put a pin in right through the bone to hold it in place. I remember the pin sticking out just a little bit further than it was supposed to, and the doctor going in and cutting it so it wouldn't protrude through the skin. Keep in mind, when I was in my body, lying on the table, I couldn't see what the doctor was doing because of the sheet erected between us. Now I could observe the entire procedure from above and to the right of my head. I could even count the stitches he had made in my hand. He took such great care in completing his work.

Time passed without me knowing how much or little had gone by. Then suddenly, the person next to me told me it was time to go. It was then that I understood I was dead, and I wasn't coming back.

And yet I still felt no fear, only peace.

Chapter 5

I t was almost like the twinkling of an eye. Suddenly, I was standing in an open field of waist-high grass, and there was something different about me. In this moment I was whole. Complete. Not only did I not feel any pain, but there was no longer any damage to my hand. In fact, any scars I'd acquired over the years were gone, any aches or pains from sports injuries were absent, and my receding hairline was now a full head of glorious hair. In a way, it was an odd sensation, like when the whir of an electric appliance suddenly shuts off. You don't realize it's a constant irritation until it's no longer there, but the relief you feel is palpable and refreshing.

As I looked around, it was difficult to process how beautiful this new place was. How do you describe things you've never experienced before—especially when you have nothing to compare them to? It's like explaining how salt tastes to someone who's never tried it. It was wholly unique. The individual elements were earthly—ground, sky, grass—but the colors and feel were beyond anything I'd ever seen or felt before. For example, the field I stood in didn't *behave* like a normal field of grass; it didn't blow with the wind. In fact, there was no wind to blow the grass, not even a breeze. Instead, it was as if each separate spring-green blade was its own entity with its own personality or soul that *chose* to flow toward me. I remember reaching my arms out to my sides and running my hands along the tops of the grass. When I did so, it was as if each individual gold-tipped blade was…somehow imparting love and acceptance to my fingertips. I could feel love coming from the grass.

While standing in the field, the guide who was with me in surgery and who had escorted me to this new place, admonished me to never look back. It was okay to look forward but not to look back.

I didn't fully understand his admonishment, but I did as he asked. Again, I couldn't see him; I could only hear his instructions in my mind. In this new place though, he was standing in a different position. I felt him near me, in the blind spot to the left and behind me. Incidentally, it was the opposite side from when we were watching the surgery. Whether it has bearing on anything, I don't know. It was just something I noted.

Taking in the view in front of me, I observed it was like standing inside a panoramic photograph. I could see a good distance to the left and a good distance to the right, but the things in front of me were more close up. Time also seemed to slow. With the slower *speed*, I noticed how minute details were easier to absorb and appreciate.

On my far left were trees, a forest of them. Giant pillars with huge trunks seemed to usher me toward what was in front of me. There were no branches on the bottom of the trunks, but I could see lots of leaves at the top, beautiful leaves in brilliant colors. The red was bright but a deep burgundy shade—similar to the color of Japanese maple leaves. The yellow color I saw was the color of yellow apples, and there were two different greens: one a spring green and the other a deeper darker green. Again, both were extremely bright, like the brightness of the colors in the aurora borealis. Also each leaf had a sort of iridescent or reflective golden underside, similar to the reflective scales on a butterfly's wings. The closest earthly equivalent I've seen to the colors I saw is probably the foliage colors of the trees in Provo Canyon in autumn, especially the color of the tree trunks.

The trunks of the trees weren't the sort of dirty brown we see here. They were a beautiful rich brown color edged in gold. I once went to Washington state in the Pacific Northwest on vacation. The closest earthly trees I've seen were those growing in the Hoh Rainforest and around the Olympic Peninsula. Being on that trip was part of the process I went through in knowing what I'd seen was real. I walked among those trees in the quiet and remembered.

Between me and the forest were tall wildflowers, about waist-high like the grass. And their colors! I've never seen colors so brilliant. They were ten to a hundred times the vibrancy of any colors we see here on Earth. Everything before me was beyond description in terms of brightness, infusion, and saturation of color. Colors we see here on Earth are dull by comparison.

Here in our earthly existence, rosebushes require a person to walk around them to see the center of each bloom, as the individual flowers face in varying directions. But looking at the wildflowers in the field, each vibrantly colored flower—and its leaves, for that matter—faced toward me. And just like the grass, the flowers radiated and communicated love. Their *faces* and leaves followed me as I progressed through the field and then seemed to encourage or propel me forward upon passing them. Having never considered the possibility of love coming from flowers, from plants, from trees, it amazed me to feel that all of it was alive, alive with a kind of love I couldn't fathom. And it gave me so much peace. It was like each individual living thing imparted an energy into me that conveyed unconditional love, support, and encouragement.

As I walked, I noticed there was no sound—no wind, no rustling of tree leaves, or flowers, no shushing of blowing grass. There were no birds chirping or sounds of water. Also the field was completely flat. There weren't any mounds of soil or the unevenness of planted rows. And unlike walking through an earthly field of waist-high grass, there was no resistance or prickliness as I proceeded forward—nothing to slow my progress as I moved through it. In fact, like the flowers, the grass and the trees all propelled me forward. They pushed and pulled as I moved along, drawing me toward what was in front of me. It felt like each living thing had its own spirit and that spirit conveyed love; it made me feel like I was special beyond compare and encouraged me ever forward.

They were all propelling me toward what was next for me—something far beyond earthly description. In front of me, three enormous clusters of puffy clouds floated in a vivid blue sky. Recently, someone showed me a photo of blue bioluminescence. I'd never seen it before, but I noticed its vibrant-blue glow was the closest thing to the blue of the sky I saw. Placed against that brilliant backdrop were the big clumps of clouds. None of the clouds moved, as there wasn't any wind. The central cloud was a magnificent cumulonimbus-like cloud unique to the other two cumulus-sized clumps. Also different from the white of the clouds on the sides, the central cloud was a brilliant pearly iridescent color that I can only describe as…pure and extremely bright, so bright that I somehow knew I wouldn't be able to look at it with human eyes. In several spots, rays burst out from the cloud toward me. The rays were, to my surprise, like the grass, trees, and flowers. They reached out to me as if to wrap themselves around me and draw me toward them. They imparted a spectacular love and energy that brought an immense sense of peace.

In this place, there was no fear, no stress, no anxiety, no judgment, and no pain. Only love and acceptance. Pure and unconditional.

Chapter 6

After taking in my new surroundings, I noticed the guide who had brought me to this place suddenly wasn't there anymore. Normally, I would expect to feel discomfort, nervousness, or even some feelings of abandonment once I realized he wasn't there. Instead, despite knowing I was alone, I felt the continued love and acceptance of everything around me, and I didn't feel fear or anxiousness—just the continual peace.

What happened next, though, is still hard for me to share. In the next instant, I found myself immersed in a replay of my life from birth to twenty-eight years old. Unlike watching a video on a screen, it was more a reliving of every moment of my life—experiencing every choice, pivotal decision, and milestone, but through the critical lens of the wisdom and maturity I attained over the course of my stunted existence. Going back, I saw how my parents raised me and reexperienced interactions with my brothers and sister. I reviewed all the activities we went to and witnessed all the time and effort my parents put into my welfare—especially the lessons they taught me—and the huge investment of time, money, and support they put into my sports.

This deep dive into my past showed me all the good things I'd done but also the bad things. With this reliving, there was no room for argument, no explanations or justifications, and no whining. It was what it was—black and white. Now I could see my actions for what they really were.

What hurt the most was how I had treated my wife in the time before I died. I wasn't very good to her. I knew she loved me and gave her all to our relationship, but on my end, everything had been about me. My time and efforts hadn't been about her or my family.

It had all been about how I could get ahead—no matter the cost to others—and how much money I could rake in. Relationships hadn't mattered unless they furthered my goals in some way. Ultimately, unless it benefitted me in the amount of money in my bank account, it wasn't worth my time. Love, compassion, and caring hardly factored into anything. I'd been living my life for me only. I'd been living my life all wrong.

This knowledge was stark to me. There were many ways I could have done better. I knew I could have done better, but I didn't.

With a life review like that, I think I expected chastisement, harsh judgment, rejection, and maybe even fear. I waited for a higher power to berate me, and punish me. How could I experience what I had in the field without understanding the paramount nature of unconditional love? And here I had conducted my life without a second thought to it. I feared the rejection, the disappointment, the wrath I was sure would come down on me like an executioner's ax.

What I did experience couldn't have been more contradictory. Instead, I felt like the prodigal. Yes, I'd made some unfortunate decisions—and I felt a deep disappointment and shame in myself because of it—but whoever had given me the opportunity to relive my life's experiences seemed to lift my chin and smile with compassion I felt I didn't deserve. Whoever this higher power was only exuded love, patience, and unconditional forgiveness.

Why?

There wasn't time to mull over much of such an impactful event. Instead, at the end of my life's reliving, a command came to move forward, toward the beautiful white cloud.

Chapter 7

The voice wasn't audible. It entered my mind, like the guide's voice. Yet it wasn't one I had heard before. It was a male voice, and I listened when it asked me to move forward.

At this point, I felt that whatever was going to happen next was reality and that I couldn't look back. I knew I was dead and considered that this was the next step in my existence—even though that existence would no longer be on Earth. And yet I felt no sorrow or remorse. I was completely calm and assured.

Walking forward in the field, I saw a sort of fog or mist-like layer that led from the grass to the cloud. As I moved toward the cloud, I felt the grass, trees, flowers, and rays of light draw me forward and up. The fog layer led me up from the field to the cloud like a short flight of stairs ascending to a stoop.

Upon approaching the cloud, an arm suddenly came through and reached toward me. At about the mid-bicep area, the arm stopped reaching toward me through the cloud. Nothing else was visible—no face or body. From observing the arm, I could tell the person on the other side of the cloud was male and larger in stature than me, taller than my six feet and three inches. And stronger. His arm and hand were bigger than mine and I weigh around 260 pounds. It looked as though His arm and hand belonged to a man involved in hard manual labor, like a man in construction work or farming.

Surprisingly, I perceived that He wasn't alone on the other side of the cloud. Understanding how I knew that is still unclear, but I did know other people were there with Him, people I couldn't see or hear. But I could sense they were there.

Often people who contact me are curious to know what color the man's skin was. The only way to describe it is that there wasn't a color at all. It was simply extremely bright. It wasn't white; it wasn't brown; it wasn't black. Describing the skin as having a color would be incorrect, as it wasn't anything but bright and pure.

When His hand reached toward me, I reached out to grasp it. I even double-reached for it, only to watch with dismay as the arm suddenly withdrew back into the cloud as suddenly as it had appeared.

The very moment before my fingers touched His though, I could feel an energy and love pass between our hands that I had only felt once before. It brought me back to a particular moment when I relived the events of my life. It was the exact moment when the nurse placed my tiny newborn body on the stomach of my mother. That purity of love is the closest thing to what I felt—the love of a mother for her newborn child. Just like the feelings of the prodigal son I'd experienced in the reliving of my life, I felt the all-consuming, pure love of a parent for their child who has finally returned home.

Then His voice entered my mind one last time. "It is not yet your time. You have more things yet to do."

I'll never forget those words. "It is not yet your time. You have more things yet to do." I never saw the hand again, and I never heard another voice.

Chapter 8

The next thing I knew, I was in my body, lying on the table as they wheeled me out of the operating room. Quite unlike feeling no pain when I left my body, upon returning, there was a great deal of pain. Laying on my chest was a death certificate, a document stating they had officially declared me dead for a duration of twenty minutes. When they wheeled me down the hall, my wife was sitting in the hallway. The doctor approached her and said, "He's okay. Everything's okay. Everything went just fine. We brought him back." Rather than bringing comfort to Connie, it frightened her. She knew nothing of the previous events. What did the doctor mean, "We brought him back"? She was completely unaware of what really happened on the other side of the operating room doors. And my death was perhaps the least notable incident as far as I was concerned.

The twenty minutes I left my body on Earth had no relevance to where I'd gone. Time meant nothing. I couldn't tell you how long it took in minutes or hours to relive my life or how long I was in the field. But I can tell you it was real, every moment of it.

For the next three days, I had the privilege of feeling total peace. Whether that was a gift or a sort of side effect, I don't know, but it was the best three days I've spent on Earth. The love I'd felt lingered and filled me with continual peace.

Periodically, the doctor would stop in and ask me questions. He told me about his experience when I suddenly wasn't dead. He informed me I'd been all over the table and thrashed around when I came back. He said it appeared there was a war being fought within my body. And he was right. I didn't want to come back. As we talked, I'd relay things that, to him, were impossible. How did I know how many stitches there were? How did I know about putting the pin in the bone? How did I know the nurse had run from the room? I'd been dead for all that time. And even if I wasn't, how did I see what was happening on the other side of the sheet? The purpose of the sheet was to keep me from observing the surgery. The doctor was kind and compassionate, a religious man, and I have nothing but good memories of his professionalism and caring nature. Often I wonder about the nurse too. I hope she didn't blame herself. What happened to me was supposed to happen. It wasn't anyone's fault; it wasn't an accident; it was supposed to happen to me.

On my third day in the hospital, a reporter from one of Utah's main television stations came to my room, hoping to interview me about my experience. I told him no. Relating my experience was something I really struggled with. I didn't want to talk about it. It was so wholly personal, so sacred. I didn't want anyone to degrade it. Over the years, I largely kept it to myself. My wife knew most, but not all of it, and my kids only knew bits and pieces. I fully intended to take it to my grave.

I know I was in a place that surpassed anything on Earth. Even today, I can recall the vibrancy of the flowers and trees and the peace I felt. But the memory that shakes me the most is of the love I felt. Was it a dream? No. Because I lived it. I see my time in the field in my mind every day. I watch what happened to me every single day.

But sharing what happened to me after I died is not my purpose. I believe that one of the "things I have yet to do" is to share what I learned from it.

Chapter 9

L ooking back, the stepping stones that blessed my life are clearly discernible. They weren't monumental to anyone but me, yet those moments and people shaped the very rebellious teenager I once was into the man I am today.

Growing up, my family lived in Ogden, Utah. In the late 1960s, its population was second only to Salt Lake City. To this day, it has the reputation of a black sheep among Utah's metropolitan areas. Honestly, even in the 1960s, it wasn't the sort of place a young person should wander the streets, but it's where fifteen-year-old me found refuge after my parents told me they were getting a divorce.

Like most kids of divorce, my parent's split had a profound effect on me. Memories of lying in bed and staring at the ceiling haunt me to this day. I remember feeling despondent and completely unmoored. Soon after my parent's announcement, I stopped going to school and found fewer…productive things to do. In my sophomore year of high school, I officially dropped out and left home.

When my father moved out, he rented an apartment near downtown Ogden. At one point, I tried to live with him, but that decision ultimately proved a mistake, as it did little to ease my loneliness. He worked two jobs and was rarely present. This resulted in my early teenaged self-seeking companionship and acceptance in less-than-ideal places. Left to my own devices, I learned to lie about being in school and, at a low point, had a perilous brush with the law—I believe it had something to do with *acquiring* the milk left on neighborhood porches by the milkman and reselling it. If it hadn't been for my dad, who vouched for me, I would've gone to jail.

Not two weeks after my near miss with incarceration, I stood on the corner of 25th Street and Orchard Avenue, wondering what I was doing with my life when a car pulled up to the curb next to me.

It was a kindly-looking couple, the Andersons. And they were offering me a job. How they knew me and knew I needed a job I didn't know, but it had to be a better path than the one I was currently on.

Soon I learned that Mr. Anderson owned a successful lumber company, and Mrs. Anderson taught at what was then called Weber State College. They had a lovely home in the foothills of Ogden and wondered if I'd be willing to help with their yard work.

Kindhearted and compassionate, the Andersons took a lost and bedraggled me under their wing. With their children freshly out of the nest, the Andersons treated me like one of their own, patiently teaching me how to landscape and instilling in me pride and exactness in my work.

Their entrance into my life couldn't have come at a better time. Both of my parents quickly remarried and had new spouses who brought several more children into their lives who, understandably, further divided their attention. If I'd felt lonely and burdensome before, this only exacerbated the issue. My father moved out of his apartment, and he and his new wife started a new life in South Ogden.

Over the next few years, the Andersons miraculously stuck with me. Mrs. Anderson taught me to work responsibly, to evaluate my performance critically, and to improve on it where needed, and she'd only introduce my work as finished when I was confident I'd done my best. She was stern and disciplined, and the perfect mentor for teenaged me. She gave me the structure and boundaries I desperately needed. Mr. Anderson, in contrast, was kindly. He would often bring me a soda and tell me to take a break, and he never let me go home hungry. Eventually, they taught me how to drive and let me use their daughter's '63 Plymouth Valiant, which I remember being hideous and powder blue. Their generosity made sure I could get safely and comfortably back and forth from my dad's new place to theirs.

Halfway through my junior year, the Andersons encouraged me to return to high school. With my father living further south, it meant I had to attend an entirely different school. Again, the kindness of others blessed my life. My previous coach at Weber High School contacted the new coach at Bonneville High. He touted my abilities and encouraged the new coach to give me a chance and let me join their team. Against all odds, the Andersons helped me successfully graduate with my class at Bonneville High, and my coaches helped me earn sports scholarships for my future.

It wasn't until some twenty years later that I learned my mother was the catalyst that brought the Andersons into my life. She had been a secretary at the college where Mrs. Anderson taught and had beseeched the Andersons to do what they could to save her wayward son. Secretly, in the wings, she had been looking out for me the whole time.

Chapter 10

I n the '60s and '70s, hitchhiking across the country was a popular—and fairly safe—means of traveling around the nation.
Car ownership was expensive, hippy culture and wanderlust sat-
urated society, and many a young man hoped to avoid being drafted
into the Vietnam War. The idea of hitchhiking across the county
appealed to me for many of the aforementioned reasons and more.

After graduating high school, I felt just as lost as I had at fifteen.
Yes, the Andersons were a blessing and a tremendous influence in
my life, but I still felt like I didn't belong anywhere. The Andersons
weren't technically my family, and my parents now had new families
of their own that demanded the vast majority of their attention.

I was eighteen now. Well, barely. But I could legally go anywhere I wanted to. And if I wanted to explore, it had to be done soon.
My goal was to hitchhike across the United States before my draft
number—which was 16—came up.

Despite earning baseball scholarships from my senior year of
high school, and a very generous offer from the Andersons to put me
through college, I walked away from it all. All I had was a backpack
with a sleeping bag tied to the bottom, five dollars stuffed in my
pocket, and a loaf of bread tucked under my arm. Equipped with
that—and a healthy dose of naivete—I stood on the side of the highway that headed east up Weber Canyon and stuck my thumb out.

It was a beautiful, clear, spring-like day. I left around noon,
and it took me the rest of that day to get from Ogden to Evanston,
Wyoming. Once there, I met a guy from the Los Angeles area in
California. He was about five feet seven, had long brown hair that
reached his shoulders, and his clothes were all dark. He carried a
bedroll with rope wrapped around it, and his language was a lot more

rough than I was used to. We were both right out of high school. As we walked, we talked about the world we lived in and the fact that the Vietnam War was on both of our minds. His draft number was 103. Neither one of us wanted to go to war. In fact, we feared it. Both wondered what the country was fighting for and wanted to escape it if we could. We hitchhiked together from Evanston to Rock Springs, Wyoming, and slept on the side of the road. It was chilly, but at least we weren't alone. We even shared the little food we had. He had crackers, and I shared my bread. When we finally got to Rock Springs, he and I decided it was too hard to get rides as a pair. People were fairly willing to pick up a single rider, but two males at the same time seemed a bit too much to ask for most. Though it was nice to have a friend and someone else to talk to, we split up in Rock Springs and went our separate ways.

From Rock Springs to Cheyenne, I felt pretty lonely and was still sleeping on the side of the road until late one night when a car stopped for me outside Cheyenne. The driver was an airman and from somewhere back east, if I remember right. In his early twenties, he had blond hair and was about the same height as me. I think he felt sorry for me, especially when he heard what my draft number was. He went totally out of his way and hid me in the back of his car, smuggling me onto the air force base in Cheyenne, where he brought me dinner and let me sleep on the floor in his room. The next morning, he took me to the Denver exit of the freeway, gave me twenty-five dollars, wished me good luck, and drove away. He was extremely kind and didn't have to do any of that. To me, when I think back on it, he was what I considered the epitome of a good military person.

It was on my way to Denver, Colorado, that the perils of hitch-hiking lived up to their reputation. Along the way, a car full of guys picked me up. I thought nothing of it. Everything had gone fine so far, and I had no reason to suspect anything different. I settled into the back seat on the passenger side and looked out the window. Suddenly, the guy next to me attacked me, throwing a hard punch to my head. While the driver veered to the shoulder, they took the twenty-five dollars the airman gave me, opened the car door, and pushed me out onto the side of the road.

Despite that, I continued toward Denver and subsequently Boulder, Colorado. Only fifteen minutes after the scuffle, a family picked me up. Their name was Udy, and they took me the rest of the way into Boulder, where they lived. They were kind and let me stay with them for a couple of days. Then they took me to an unemployment office so I could fill out a resume because I was completely broke.

The unemployment office quickly set me up with a local man who owned a farm in Lamar, Colorado. It didn't take long for the farmer to discover I may have exaggerated a few things on my resume. He quickly realized my tractor-driving abilities were severely lacking. In fact, I'd never done it before. I tried to fudge a bit by telling him I'd only driven John Deere tractors and that's why I was having such a hard time with his big-wheeled red-and-yellow Versatile, but I think he had my number. Luckily, I think my work ethic won him over.

Not long after hiring me, the farmer put me to work on his farm in Tribune, Kansas. He assigned an unfortunate farmhand to show me the ropes. He had the unenviable task of teaching me how to drive the tractor. Standing behind me, perched on the back of the tractor, he showed me what all the knobs and gears did. When I tried to do it myself, I put the throttle on too fast, and the front wheels of the tractor came up off the ground, throwing the farmhand off the back of the tractor and down into the dirt. Fortunately, he dusted himself off and patiently kept working with me until I could drive well and make all my lines on the field straight. Soon I was pretty proud of my work, until one day when I didn't make a corner sharp enough and took out the guy wire for the power line. Everyone in the surrounding area found themselves in a blackout. I hightailed it out of the field and hurried back to the farm. That night, I went to the small highway gas station in the area to get something to eat. All the locals were talking about the power outage. I remember nervously asking if they'd found the person responsible. They told me no, but that they were sure they'd find them soon. I hurried out of there pretty quick.

Another incident happened when it was harvest time on the farm. My job was to drive a truck with a big trailer on it. A combine would reap, thresh, gather, and winnow the wheat and shoot the grain into the trailer I pulled. That part wasn't so hard, but when I got to the grainery to deliver the wheat, I had no idea what I was supposed to do. After waiting in the long line of trucks ready to deliver their loads, it came my turn. Having never delivered grain, I didn't know you were supposed to dump the grain slowly while inching forward. Completely clueless, I dumped the entire trailer load all at once, burying the men overseeing the grainery up to their waists. Not only did it anger them, but the long line of truck drivers behind me would suffer extended delays in getting back to the fields. That lost time equaled a loss of money. I don't think there was a person who wasn't angry at me that day. From then on, I learned from my mistake and did it right going forward.

Had I not learned the discipline and intense work ethic from the Andersons, I know I wouldn't have done as well as I did on the farm. Their influence helped me learn how to work hard, be persistent, and gain pride in a job well done.

Four months spent on a farm really gave a lost eighteen-year-old kid a lot of valuable life lessons. One of the best things the farmer taught me was to appreciate a day of rest. On the farm, you worked twelve hours a day, seven days a week unless you went to church. If you went to church, you could have Sundays off. Growing up, my family was semireligious, but the older I got, the less it mattered. Going to church in Kansas changed that. Even though the church I attended in Kansas wasn't the one I went to as a kid, I relished the opportunity to go. It was then that I learned to appreciate the scriptures. It was the first time they meant something special to me. They brought me peace I couldn't get anywhere else.

The nights in the bunkhouse were so quiet. It left a lot of unwanted time focusing on my future and goals. It created a bunch of worry about what would happen to me if I went to war. When I first arrived on the farm, I called home to let my dad know where I was. On that call, he informed me there was a letter from Uncle Sam waiting on the kitchen table. My draft number was up.

In September, the seasonal work on the farm ended, and I had to decide what to do next. Having saved some money by that point, I could resume traveling. I decided against continuing east because fall and winter were right around the corner. California seemed like a good idea during the cold months, so I started west. I only got as far as Ogden. I was in Utah less than twenty-four hours before the authorities picked me up in a grocery store parking lot. That night they sent me to Salt Lake City, where they inducted me into the army. By the next afternoon, I was in Fort Leonard Wood, Missouri, for basic training.

Chapter II

I t occurs to me that mentioning terms like draft numbers and the Vietnam War may not mean much to people of other countries or generations. With that in mind, I hope you'll forgive an opportunity to share some context. Through roughly the 1960s and the first half of the '70s, the United States found itself involved in what they officially named the Vietnam conflict. It was a war. There is a ton of debate about whether the United States should have inserted itself. Getting into the weeds and the politics of the thing is not my aim here. I merely wish to convey the mood of young American men during that era, as that is what I experienced.

In some countries, then and now, young men are required to enter military service when they reach adulthood. It isn't a requirement in the United States. Young men, instead, sign up for the draft at eighteen years old. This essentially means our military has a contingency plan. If it's short of troops, or enters a war, the young men signed up for the draft can then be called up to serve their country. It's officially termed the Selective Service System. According to the Selective Service System website, the draft was in use from the years 1917 to 1973, with the singular exception of the year 1947. As of 1973, the draft has lain dormant, thus allowing young Americans to go about their lives without a looming threat.

The website for the United States' National Archives lists the final Vietnam War US military fatal casualty count at 58,220. The year I graduated, 1971, the death rate of US troops showed small signs of slowing. Unfortunately, by that time, the country had a pretty horrific picture of what was happening in Vietnam. Most young men, like me, felt that when their draft number came up, it was the beginning of the end. Being sent to Vietnam was the death knell.

Arriving at basic training, draftees understood they scheduled everyone to go to Vietnam. It was simply a matter of time until you shipped out. Walking around with that kind of ticking time bomb on your shoulders left a giant gangrenous foot in the door for depression, despair, resentment, anger, hopelessness, you name it. Sports again became my refuge. Basketball was the flavor of the month as the weather got cooler. As it was, every weekend was an opportunity to head to the gym and shake off some cares. You didn't know who you were playing against; it was a time to just play and not think about anything else. At the time, I was so angry. I just wanted to play to forget my precarious circumstances.

It wasn't long, though, before I discovered some guys I was playing with and against were NBA basketball players and high-quality college ballers. It felt great to know I could hold my own.

One fateful weekend, the sergeant major who was over the basketball team for the base at Fort Leonard Wood came up to me and asked if I'd like to try out for the base team. Back then it was called the Continental League. I told him no. I wasn't interested. When it came to my forced military service, I just wanted to get in, get out, and move on with my life. He walked away, and I got back in the game, although it was hard to focus when I noticed him watching me. About a week later, I came back and played again. Again, the sergeant major petitioned me with the same question. I gave him the same answer: I wanted to get my military service over with, get out, and get on with my life. The third time he approached me, he said something that stopped me in my tracks. "Before you say anything, Private, I want to tell you where your orders are." Then he informed me they had slated my unit for the front lines in Vietnam. "I'm not going to ask you again," he said, "but I'd like you to play if you want to." Finding out I had orders to go to the front lines left no question in my mind. I summarily volunteered to play basketball.

The rest of my unit went to Vietnam. I stayed at the base and played basketball. From what I understand, I was one of three from my group that went home alive. My unit was wiped out. Sports rescued me like it had after my parents' divorce. And what a tremendous gift that was to me.

After my time at Fort Leonard Wood in basic training and AIT, they asked me where I wanted to go, and I said, "Please, anywhere but Vietnam." They sent me to Karlsruhe, Germany. There, I worked as a postal worker. I was a 75B. That's what they called it. It was a clerical job.

Despite being in Germany, a month didn't go by that we weren't on alert to have our bags packed and ready to go to Vietnam. It made us focus on sharpening the skills we learned in basic training. Yet it never freed us from the fear of the Vietnam guillotine ever looming heavily over everyone's heads.

In Germany, I continued to play basketball for the army. I even got drafted to play basketball for a German club. But that wasn't the highlight of my time there. About a year into my assignment in

Germany, the Lord sent my greatest blessing. I was in Pforzheim and ended up playing basketball with a friend who'd shipped out with me from Salt Lake City. He was married to a girl from his hometown and suggested introducing me to his wife's sister, who was visiting from the states. She was a lively, blonde-haired, blue-eyed American girl named Connie. She was petite and had a smile like sunshine. I fell instantly in love. We met in June and were engaged after only three weeks. In July, I got permission to take Connie back to the states. We were married in September and returned to Germany together. Out of all the tremendous blessings I received after entering the military, that was by far the sweetest.

Around the last month of my military service, Connie and I returned to the states. There I switched things up and played for the all-army baseball team at Fort Indiantown Gap, Pennsylvania.

1975 brought two notable events: one, the blessed birth of our first child, and two, my joyous release from the army with an honorable discharge, my dog tags, and DD214.

ARMY SOFTBALL TEAM (1973–1975)

73-75 KARLSRUHE, GERMANY

The 1972-73 Ft. Wood Hilltoppers basketball team, front row, left to rig
Bobby Williamson, Pat McNally, Juiel Chappel, Tim Carlson, Gor
Tunision, Dan Rainey, Robert Reed. Back row, left to right: coach T
Parker, Marvin Drummond, Murry Mills, Jeff Perkins, Bill Benford, I
Mueller, Dan Bivens, Brian Katt.   (Guide Staff Ph

ARMY BASKETBALL TEAM IN GERMANY (1975)

Chapter 12

Following my release from the army, I found the skills I learned in the service transferred smoothly to civilian life. The United States Postal Service seemed an obvious career choice due to my assignment in the army, so I applied, got the job, and started working there right away. Connie appreciated that it gave us a steady paycheck every two weeks, provided insurance, and built a retirement. At the time—I admit—I wanted to push further, reach higher. It was hard to keep my focus on putting in the time when my natural drive was to aim for something bigger and brighter that made a lot more money.

Hoping to continue pursuing sports, I tried to play basketball at the collegiate level but found my time playing club ball in Germany disqualified me from competing on a college team. Baseball, on the other hand, was still available to me, so I went after and got a spot playing for the baseball team at Brigham Young University.

While attending BYU, the Post Office demanded more and more of my time, and eventually, I had to leave BYU to fulfill all the Post Office asked me to do—even though I had nearly enough credits to graduate. Soon I began working all over the country for the PO, which took me away from home often. My drive as an athlete, my military training, and the work ethic I retained from the Andersons as a young man pushed me to overachieve and excel at work.

Unfortunately, on this upward climb, the drive to get ahead professionally, feel successful, and make a lot of money quickly consumed my every thought and action. Everything I did was for myself, and I had little care or concern for my growing family—other than knowing the money I made fed, housed, and clothed them.

The Post Office was more than obliging when it came to keeping my ego fed and pushing me to succeed. They sent me on assignments all over the country to audit Post Offices, set up new programs, write manuals in Washington D.C., and teach postal rate increases. In no time at all, I was a manager in over six states. All this equaled more time away from home and didn't bother me in the least. Pursuing my goals was paramount. That fact made it easy to forget my wife was basically operating as a single mother.

Thinking back, my favorite assignment by far was auditing Post Offices all over Hawaii, for obvious reasons. The most harrowing assignment was in Watts, California. At the time, the Los Angeles riots were razing downtown Los Angeles and safety was a concern. The Postal Service issued me a sidearm, told me to be out of the office by 4:00 p.m., and advised me to roll through every stoplight for safety.

All that meant I was away from home for weeks at a time. The relationships I cultivated were those at work. I could relate to the postmasters I worked with and made a lot of good friends, but it all came at a huge cost to my marriage.

On the short stints I had at home, I spent my time playing adult-league sports instead of spending time with my wife and children. My momentum and drive had to be fed. At one of my lowest points, I paid no heed as my wife sat on the bleachers at my baseball game while in the beginning stages of labor with our daughter. And she wasn't just in a delicate health situation; she had to keep track of our other children while cheering for me. Other guys on the team really worried about her and checked on her regularly, but my attention was laser-focused on winning the game.

Just before my near-death experience, the Post Office sent me to a middle-of-nowhere town called Jackpot, Nevada, for stretches of three weeks at a time. When I finally went home for some rare time off, I didn't spend it at home with my young family. Instead, on that fateful New Year holiday, I went skiing with a friend.

It's no wonder it took an act of God to snap me out of myself.

Before you worry I'll spend pages harping in self-castigation, I'll say that the Post Office was very good to me. They trusted my abilities and basically let me run my offices of responsibility for thirty years of duty. Job security was never an issue for me, and I got a tremendous amount of satisfaction knowing I had a steady income to support my family. We never went without, and I had the opportunity to work with so many dedicated people along the way.

It wasn't until after my NDE that I realized life was not about the mighty dollar or how high I could climb the ladder. I had missed the entire point! In the next life, relationships, knowledge, and the opportunities taken to serve your fellow men go with you. Riches, accolades, and fame get left behind. They. Do. Not. Matter. And all the people you hurt along the path to get ahead, all the relationships you neglect, and all the opportunities to help your fellow men that you dismiss are viewed in your life's review. You suddenly realize that society's expectations are grossly inverse.

The goal in sharing my near-death experience after so many years is to show and teach people how to get a better life's review. I guess you could say it's like a tutorial. And since it's obvious by now that I'm ultracompetitive, it should be clear that I'm serious about wanting to help others achieve the highest levels—get the best review possible. Of course, I don't know each individual's situation, and can't comprehend the trials that some are asked to endure. I'm not claiming to understand. All I wish to do is impart my knowledge, help lift and encourage others, and show them that dying is nothing to fear.

In the following chapters, I hope to impart the core lessons I've learned from dying. Keep in mind, I have never claimed to know everything. I'm no prophet. I'm imperfect. And I mess up all the time. The point is to keep going, keep trying. I know that God loves effort. He wants you to succeed a thousand times more than even I do. My hope is that you'll take this advice for what it's worth and customize it to your unique situation. There are people out there who need you. There are also people out there—both in heaven and on Earth—who are hoping, waiting, encouraging, and supporting you. Just give this advice a chance. It's changed my life. It's brought happiness and meaning and doesn't cost anything but the honest effort you're able to put forth.

Chapter 13

P eople often ask me why, after forty long years of silence, I decided to share my experience. To be honest, I fully intended to take it to my grave. Through the years, I told my wife bits and pieces of the story, but my children knew even less. It simply wasn't something I wanted to share.

For me, my experience is sacred, not secret but sacred. I have never wanted it bandied about or sensationalized; I never wanted to see it cheapened or mocked. It wasn't until I met Wes Lapioli that I could see an important alternate perspective.

Wes lives in my neighborhood. We see each other occasionally on the river walk that runs near our houses. During the COVID-19 lockdowns, it was a popular place for people to get out in the fresh air without breaking any rules.

Before COVID, Wes had a job in tech. He hated it. He dreaded going to work every morning and felt the opportunity to get into his dream career slipping away. What he yearned to do was create art through film and put his schooling in counseling to good use. He just didn't know how. Wes prayed in desperation. Then just when he couldn't stand going into his soul-draining job one more day, he received an answer to his prayer—albeit a vague one. The Spirit whispered to Wes that "everything was going to change." Although he didn't fully understand the message, Wes went forward in faith, hoping he would know what to do when the time was right.

Somewhere along the line, Wes heard me mention I wasn't afraid to die. That statement both fascinated and stuck with him. After further prayer and pondering, he felt the Spirit tell him, "You need to help him." Then COVID descended on the world, and Wes lost his much-despised job. Happy to be free from his everyday grind but still too nervous to approach me, Wes sat down and decided to prioritize his life. He knew the Lord loves effort, so he sat down and made lists, prayed, and went forward again in faith.

Not long after, a blessing came to Wes when he and I crossed paths on the neighborhood river walk. He knew the opportunity wasn't coincidental and finally submitted to the divine push he felt to ask if he could help me. At the time, I was less than interested in talking about my experience. Again, it was something I'd never fully discussed with anyone, and never planned to. Then when I realized he meant for me to share it in a filmed interview, I said no. Over time, Wes persisted, and I think I told him "no" a few more times. Finally, he suggested I talk to Connie about the idea and to pray about it. He felt that because of the ravages of COVID, there were many people whom my story could help. He thought it might give hope and help those who were fearing death, COVID, and dealing with the loss of loved ones.

When Connie and I discussed it, she thought Wes might be right. She wondered if maybe the time had come to share. I was still very reluctant, but we agreed to pray about the idea and then get back to Wes after a few days.

Something profound happened when I knelt and asked God if what Wes was proposing was something I should do. My answer was clear, and I'll never forget it. The Spirit said, "It's about the one."

I pondered on that answer for quite a while. What exactly did that mean? Deciding to study it out, I listened to many inspirational messages, searched scriptures, and prayed some more. The idea was definitely not a novel concept to me. It was something I had adopted after my experience with death, but I wanted to more fully under-stand what God wanted me to do when it came to speaking with Wes about my experience.

There is a scripture in the King James Version of the New Testament in the Bible that really stood out as I studied. It's in the book of Luke, chapter 15, verses 3 through 7. It reads:

> And he spake this parable unto them, saying,
> What man of you, having an hundred
> sheep, if he lose one of them, doth not leave the

ninety and nine in the wilderness, and go after that which is lost, until he find it?

And when he hath found *it*, he layeth *it* on his shoulders rejoicing.

And when he cometh home, he calleth together *his* friends and neighbours, saying unto them, Rejoice with me; for I have found my sheep which was lost.

I say unto you, that likewise joy shall be in heaven over one sinner that repenteth, more than over ninety and nine just persons, which need no repentance.

If you've ever watched the film *The Chosen*, there is a scene in season 2, episode 1, where Jesus is explaining to a gathered crowd what he means by this scripture in terms the people of that time could understand.

JESUS: Because we know that God pursues the sick more than the healthy. Think of it this way. Are there any sheepherders in the crowd?

SHEPHERD: I am.

JESUS: Ah, welcome! We are honored you are here. I have a very warm place in My heart for shepherds. Who is tending your flock now?

SHEPHERD: My brother. We're taking turns.

JESUS: How many sheep?

SHEPHERD: One hundred, Teacher.

JESUS: Say one of them goes astray, what would you do?

SHEPHERD: I'd go look for it, of course.

JESUS: Of course. But what about the other ninety-nine?

SHEPHERD: I'd have to leave them behind. I can't lose one sheep.

JESUS: Hmm…and if you find it?

SHEPHERD: I'd lay it over my shoulders and bring it home. And I would probably do a little dance!

(*Laughter*)

JESUS: And what would you say to your friends who are worried for you?

SHEPHERD: "Rejoice with me. I have found my lost sheep!"

JESUS: Do you see what he just said there? He rejoices more for one sheep than over the ninety-nine who never went astray. So it is not the will of My Father that one of these should perish. In the same way, I tell you, there will be more joy in heaven over one sinner who repents than over ninety-nine righteous persons who need no repentance.

Come

Come is not alone, it's with someone. Come is not demand, it is gentle persuasion. Come is open arms, not pointing fingers. Come is never giving up, my hope still lingers. Come unto the Shepherd, my lonely child, for He is calling after you. "Come follow me," hear Him call you, I will seek out all my sheep, I will deliver them. Hear Him call you, leaving the ninety-nine, I will find you my little one. Come follow me, see His open arms. He is waiting... For you.

Poem written by Debbie Beckstrom

If you happen to be a parent, or spouse, or sibling, or uncle, or aunt, or friend, it's easy to see how you could apply the same concept. If your child, or spouse, or sibling, or family member, or friend was in crisis, you would do everything in your power to help them. And then rejoice when all was well again.

What I now understand is that our aid to others isn't limited to our close group of family members and friends; it encompasses every child of God. Every neighbor, colleague, and stranger—at times—is the one.

Does this mean we go about meddling in the lives of everyone around us? No, it means we help when and where it's needed *if* we have either the physical, mental, emotional, and/or financial ability to serve. Often, only listening ears, smiling mouths, or compassionate hands are required.

What are some examples of the one?

It's the lady in the grocery store who is counting her meager change to buy the five items in her cart to feed her small children. Be observant. Pay for her food. Get out of your comfort zone and do it when you get the prompting.

The one might be a neighbor you feel compelled to talk to. Don't judge him by his outward appearance. Leave your insecurity behind and get to know his heart. Be a true friend. Be there when he has a loss in his family. Offer to walk his dog when he's sick and can't do it himself. Good neighbors often become eternal friends.

On a lazy Saturday, when you come out of Home Depot and someone is struggling to load things into their vehicle, listen to that Still Small Voice that prompts you. Stop and help a new friend.

When you're online, make an effort to be kind. There are more than enough trolls out there. Be a person who is friendly, supportive, and genuinely concerned. You never know when someone is struggling, lonely, or having thoughts of suicide. Your kind words and sincere caring may be the thing that changes their day/week/life. Pay attention to the rush you feel from bringing hope and light to someone in darkness and despair.

So after pondering and studying all these things—and after forty years of silence—I felt that the power of prayer led me to know it was now time to share my story. It was time for me to reach out to the one. I contacted Wes and told him I was willing, and more than twenty million views on YouTube later, the message has resonated all over the world. Prayer and following promptings made that happen, not me, not Wes—the Spirit, Jesus Christ, and God.

I live for the peace I felt during and after the incident, so I feel that if I can share it with others and offer even a modicum of peace to them, it's worth sharing what I experienced.

Chapter 14

When the opportunity comes to make a change in your life, finding a good mentor can be the difference between success and failure. Now that you've read about my early years of life, it's obvious that the intervention of good people played a major role in helping a lost and broken teenager get on the right path. If you aren't in a place mentally or emotionally to mentor others, find a mentor/doctor/therapist/friend and heal yourself quickly. But when you're ready, helping others—with the side benefit of getting outside your own head and problems—is surprisingly healing. Service to others can even produce a high. It can fill your soul with peace and light that soothes all kinds of hurts and is the best kind of addicting.

From *Dictionary.com*:
mentor [men-tawr, -ter]
noun
1. a wise and trusted counselor or teacher
2. an influential senior sponsor or supporter

Marrying Connie brought tremendous blessings I never could have anticipated. One of those surprising gifts was a man who became my greatest mentor: her father, Joe Warner. The effect he had on my life was profound and everlasting. I owe so much of who I am today to him.

I think Aesop had it right when he said good things come in small packages. Spending a good portion of my time around high-level basketball players, and being six feet three myself, Joe—who was barely five feet six—might've been considered small for a man. But to me, he was a giant among men.

45

Joe came from a rich heritage of men who exemplified honor, compassion, and integrity—traits I didn't even realize I was desperate to learn and emulate. In 1917, Joe's grandfather, Milo Warner, built Warner's Garage. Not many years later, the garage was among some of the first Ford dealerships formed in the western states. The garage sold the first Model T's in their area. Over its long and distinguished existence, six generations of Joe's family worked in that dealership until it was sold a few years after his death in 2011. Joe never retired and his family often joked that he would die sitting at his desk at *the garage*. His work ethic was incredible and the dealership earned multiple awards from Ford Motor Company.

Though Joe's business acumen was admirable, it was only one small facet of his many laudable traits. For Joe, his word and a handshake were stronger than any legal document, all people were equal and valued, and I've never met another man who held his wife up on a pedestal the way Joe did.

I grew up in a home where no one said the words "I love you," and physical affection wasn't something you considered engaging in. Maybe some of you can relate to this, and others can't, but for me, the way Joe engaged with his family was utterly foreign. Every time he saw you, he made sure you heard him say he loved you, he freely offered hugs and kisses, and he showed a genuine interest in and focus on whomever he engaged in conversation with. I couldn't help but watch and be amazed by the way he lived his life and presided over his family. He was the very epitome of a valiant patriarch.

His front porch was the scene of many a learning opportunity. Politics and war stories were the only taboo topics of discussion (Joe was a WWII veteran), but the knowledge imparted there soaked into my heart and mind, and I'll never forget those lessons. They taught me how to be a better father, how to love my wife, and that every human life was precious.

There was a story told about a farming family in Joe's rural Utah community. Being a farming family, they didn't have much, but what they had in abundance was something you can't buy with money. Tragically, their son needed care from a specialist in San Francisco. This family had a good farm truck, but it was hardly something they could rely on to get them the 726 miles needed to get them from their farm to San Francisco. In small rural communities, there is no Hertz, or Budget, or Enterprise to rent a reliable vehicle from. And even if there were, this humble family was strapped by mounting medical bills for their son. Joe didn't hesitate and stepped in and offered one of the dealership vehicles for this family to travel to San Francisco for the needed treatment.

Joe was just that kind of man. He remembered everyone's names and knew their personal stories but never spoke an unkind word about anyone. He taught me to be a caring father, to respect others no matter their station or circumstances, and to be a good husband. I learned to observe and emulate the master. His wasn't a forced or coerced teaching either. He taught me by quiet example.

In the thirty-seven years of my marriage while he was on the earth, he taught so many time-honored lessons: love your wife; be an example to your children and grandchildren; be mindful of others' needs; use your mind—that's something you can take with you when you die; when you commit to doing a task, do it, and do it the best you can. He, like the Andersons, taught me how important it was to finish the job.

Joe always had what we called a *Hollywood* smile on his face. He knew how to make someone's day brighter. He taught me that material things don't make happiness—happiness comes within the soul. He had a knack for making everyone feel they were the most important person on the planet. And if he shook your hand and called you "a gentleman and a scholar," that was the highest of compliments.

He loved his wife, Madge, more than anything in the world. He carried her around on a pillow. She was his queen. That's something I still strive to emulate. His example in that department is a tough act to follow.

Joe was a man who believed in using his mind. He was not a physical person, but his mind was brilliant. I remember him learning a new word from the dictionary every day. At his Ford dealership, he probably gave more cars away than he sold. He watched out for others and served in many community leadership capacities.

I couldn't have had a better example in my lifetime.

One of my favorite memories of Joe was an annual Ford Motor Company Golf Tournament. It was a four-man scramble with eighteen holes. Joe asked me to bring a friend and play along with him and his wife, Madge. It was held at a picturesque golf course at Jeremy Ranch in Park City, Utah.

Joe and Madge had never played golf. Jeremy Ranch was a spectacular, professional course played on the Senior Tour. My friend, Craig Slack, and I knew we had to play our best to compete in this tournament, so the odds were that we didn't have a chance at winning. To start the tournament, each person hit a drive, and the longest drive got used. For the next shot, all four players tried to hit a shot to the green, but as per tournament rules, you used the best shot. If it was on the putting green, you would putt from the closest point to the flagpole. On the greens, Madge and Joe would putt first; that way Craig and I could read the bends, speed, and breaks to the hole.

Both Craig and I soon learned how important this event was to Joe. As the tournament proceeded, and after the first nine holes, we felt we were actually playing well enough to contend in the tournament. A fun day on the links now became an honest-to-goodness fight to win.

In the final nine holes, our luck continued to hold. One of the pinnacle moments was watching Joe sink a twenty-foot putt. I watched Joe become a champion golfer before my eyes!

He was so much fun to watch. He got so excited about a sport that is really not easy to play. Between Craig and I, we taught Joe how to enjoy the game. But he taught us even greater lessons. He would point out all the things sportsmen might overlook, things like the beauty of the environment we were playing in and how grateful he was that the winter had blessed us with enough water to maintain a beautiful golf course. He taught us to pause and appreciate life's beauties.

Yes, we had a great day golfing. Yes, we won the golf tournament. But, I won much, much more. I won lessons for life from my mentor. He taught me what was important—and it wasn't winning the tournament.

Need a mentor? Look among your peers and your circle of influence. Were you military? Was there someone you looked up to whom you could strive to emulate? Is there a neighbor, local religious leader, or friend who strikes you as a person you admire? Watch them. Talk to them. Learn from them.

If you have a good mentor, great! Now become one yourself. Look for someone or a group of someones to help and influence for good.

After my NDE, I took every opportunity to coach kids' sports. It was important to me to pay forward the kindness that others had offered me so many years ago. Looking into the faces of some of those kids, I could see my own childhood reflected back at me. Some of them really struggled and only needed one person who cared.

That's something we all need: someone who cares. Even if you don't believe in God, I know He cares. I know He watches you, hopes for you, cheers for you, and understands the things no one else can truly understand about you.

SCOTT GOLFING WITH MENTOR, JOE WARNER (SEPTEMBER 1991)

SCOTT'S MENTOR, JOE WARNER

Chapter 15

Dean Smith was the best men's college basketball coach in the country when I played ball for the army. Everyone in basketball knew his name. He was the head coach for the North Carolina Tar Heels from 1961 to 1997, and by the end of his career, he was officially the most successful men's college basketball coach of all time, leading his team to eleven trips to the Final Four and scoring two NCAA (National Collegiate Athletic Association) championships. His title as the men's college basketball coach with the most career victories stood unmatched until 2007. He also coached who is arguably the greatest basketball player of all time: Michael Jordan.

As if that wasn't enough to garner admiration, Dean Smith's plethora of achievements included election to the Basketball Hall of Fame and coaching the US men's basketball team to win Olympic gold in 1976.

I admit I really wanted—and came close to having—Dean Smith as a coach. In fact, at the beginning of 1975, my dreams of playing in the Olympics held the spark of becoming a reality.

As a soldier in the army, patriotism becomes a new intrinsic part of your existence. Average Americans are raised with a healthy love of country, but preparing to serve and protect your homeland with your very life tends to lend an additional passion to one's devotion. A natural extension to military service, for many military personnel, is representing and competing for the United States in the Olympic Games. Next to fighting to protect, competing to honor ranks high in national achievement. Being in the army and playing basketball for them consequently created a strong desire in me to represent the United States in basketball at the Summer Olympics.

Currently, the US sends its best and brightest professional basketball players to the Olympics. That practice began in 1992 with the aptly dubbed "Dream Team," which consisted of legendary pro players: Earvin "Magic" Johnson, Michael Jordan, Larry Bird, David Robinson, Patrick Ewing, Karl Malone, Charles Barkley, John Stockton, Scottie Pippen, Christian Laettner, Clyde Drexler, and Chris Mullin. But prior to that year, the country only allowed its top amateur basketball players to compete. As soon as I found out they were accepting entries for the 1976 Summer Games, I knew I wanted to send in an entry. Training became more intense than it had ever been before. I needed to be able to play at the next level. Running, jumping, dribbling skills, and endurance all needed to improve as well as my ability to work through any pain I felt. Thankfully, some of those skills were already part of my training due to my time in the army.

From time to time, while I was stationed in Germany, our military base team would play against the German club teams. At one point, after our army team played a good game against a club team in Southern Germany, I was asked to play for their club team. On German club teams, you were allowed two Americans on a team, and only one American could play on the court at a time. My timing was good. One of the American club players got drafted into the ABA (American Basketball Association 1967–1976), which left an available spot with the German club. Playing for the army, and playing club ball for the German team, was a huge honor for me. It was exciting and something I really enjoyed. What I didn't know was that playing for the German club team was effectively disqualifying me from any chance at playing in the Olympics. American players got paid to play for the German teams. By accepting money for the club team, it categorized me as a professional basketball player, consequently prohibiting me from playing with amateurs in the Olympics. Not only did I lose my opportunity to play, but I also wouldn't be coached by Dean Smith and wouldn't be a member of the team that ultimately won Olympic gold medals in the 1976 Summer Games.

Dean Smith once said, "What you do with a mistake: recognize it, admit it, learn from it, forget it."

One can replace the word *mistake* with many other examples: lost opportunity, failure, pain, trials, and grudges.

My dream of competing in the Olympics could not be fulfilled, but playing all over Europe was a dream come true that ultimately saved me from the front lines of the Vietnam War and probable death. When it comes down to it, how could I wish that gift away?

Adjusting my ambitions and looking forward led to a desire for a career playing basketball in the NBA (National Basketball Association) at the completion of my military service. It seemed a natural vocational choice at the conclusion of my time playing ball for the army and the German club. Yet in the course of playing club ball, I broke my left foot two times and my right foot once. Due to my injuries, I wouldn't be able to pass the physical requirements for the NBA.

With my plans for a career in basketball thwarted, it would have been so easy to dwell on the could-have-beens. Basketball—and sports in general—were everything to me. With the Olympic Games out of reach, and dreams of the NBA squashed, I needed a new direction.

Alexander Graham Bell is credited with saying, "When one door closes, another one opens, but we so often look so long and so regretfully upon the closed door, that we do not see the ones which open for us."

Claiming I took all those challenges and disappointments in stride wouldn't be accurate. For most of us, it isn't easy to let go of lifelong dreams and goals. But had I dwelt too long on lost opportunities, I would have missed the new door that opened for me—the door to one of my greatest gifts. It was at this crossroad in my life that I met my wife, Connie.

Don't get me wrong; career goals are very important. They shape so much of our present and future. But at the opening of this new door, I had a companion to share that uncharted territory with, someone to walk beside me through ambitious new goals, difficult-to-make decisions, and unknown outcomes. We would get to explore them together. Now I wasn't alone. There was a person in the world just for me. That's a huge deal to someone who'd basically been on their own since the age of fifteen. It's true that a career would last me for the rest of my life, especially when you include the retirement I'd earn from it, but Connie was, and still is, my eternity. My everything. Had I gone on to the Olympics, or the NBA, I never would have met her.

I've spent a good portion of time considering the admonishment I received from my guide when he told me to never look back. Was his directive a literal instruction, or merely symbolic? I think probably both. Where I can only begin to understand the depth of the literal instruction, my grasp of the symbolic grows every day.

People often press me about my life's reliving, specifically about any judgment, anger, or punishment I might have felt after reexperiencing all the mistakes I made. While I don't know each individual's particular concern, the impression I get from most people is that they fear looking back at their lives and suffering some kind of resulting chastisement or wrath from a higher power. In my experience, this couldn't be further from the truth. When people broach the subject, I feel their remorse, their uncertainty, their regret. But that's just it: after your life's review, that's all there is: *your* own remorse, *your* own regret, *your* own disappointment. No part of that comes from God. Is it a time to face up to your mistakes? Yes. Is it an opportunity to own your actions? Yes. Does it provide certainty that you'll be judged in the only perfect way? Yes. Does it immediately remind you and leave you with a sure knowledge that God is fair, loving, forgiving, and merciful? Absolutely.

This is what the King James Version of the New Testament in the Bible says about leaving the past behind:

> Brethren, I count not myself to have apprehended: but this one thing *I do,* forgetting those things which are behind, and reaching forth unto those things which are before,
> I press toward the mark for the prize of the high calling of God in Christ Jesus. (Philippians 3:13–14)

In these verses, Paul, in the simplest way I can explain, advises us not to look back but to keep pushing forward. He's explaining that if we honestly own up to our mistakes, there is no reason to look back. Our focus should be on looking forward and beginning now to do and be better.

I agree with Paul. Don't worry about the past. Don't look back. Own up to your mistakes. Decide to be better today. Look forward. Go forward.

Chapter 16

Living in the present was, and is, a concept I feel I have to work to master every day. In the past, my natural instincts were always to aim for the future and chase goals and dreams in sports and in my career. My time in the military reinforced pushing past limits and preparing for inevitable conflicts. Therefore, slowing down long enough to enjoy a moment wasn't something I contemplated or practiced. Forward momentum was key to achieving greatness.

It wasn't just that I couldn't lose momentum either. I didn't understand why everyone else wasn't just as driven, just as hungry for what I thought were the greatest successes in life.

Steve Young's accomplishments in sports are mind-boggling. He's a two-time NFL MVP, a Super Bowl MVP, and a first-ballot Hall of Famer, just to name a few things. I don't know him personally, but I did meet him once. He and I both competed in sports for BYU, though not at the same time and not in the same sport. When I met him, he came off as a very humble man who respected others. Recently, I read something he said, and it really struck me:

> Even if we understand the idea that we should love people, we sometimes think we're supposed to love them back onto our path instead of respecting their own journey. I'm not trying to love people into coming with me. I'm just loving people. No expectations, no transaction. They and God will figure out their journey; my job is to love them along the way.

His statement was so powerful to me and goes right along with what I've been striving to learn since my life's reliving.

I remember a particular occasion when I challenged myself to work on this difficult-for-me trait; I decided to take a walk around our neighborhood and test myself. Could I simply enjoy the walk? Could I turn my drive for personal success off temporarily and look for someone else who might need unconditional kindness?

At the time, we lived in a neighborhood with newer homes. This meant everyone was a new resident, and we were all strangers to each other. The surrounding community wasn't an area where families had lived for generations, where children had grown up together, and where bonds were strong. We were all newbies.

Some people have the sort of personality that compels them to make new-neighbor gifts and cheerily introduce themselves. I'd consider myself a pretty congenial guy, but that wasn't my style. Putting myself out there in a place that wasn't directly affecting my life goals was foreign and uncomfortable, but I was determined to try.

Not too long into my walk, I felt a prompting. I abruptly felt compelled to strike up a conversation with the young guy whose house I was passing. Knowing this prompting was exactly what I had asked for, I put myself out there and said hi. He was a younger man—in his twenties probably—and stuck out in a neighborhood of typical suburban families. He was a single lanky kid with a mohawk who looked like life hadn't been easy on him. My simple introduction caught him off guard. Come to find out, in all the time he'd been in the neighborhood, not one person had ever come to talk to him.

Now is it fair to condemn the whole neighborhood for their unfriendliness? I don't think so. Again, everyone has their own story, their own journey. Some aren't in a place to put themselves out there yet. Some are unsure what to say. And yes, some are judgmental. But. I also think outward appearances can sometimes be defense mechanisms—outer shells that warn would-be attackers away. Was a rough outward exterior a defense mechanism for my neighbor? I don't know. It just goes to my point. We don't know where people are coming from. But God does. He knew this neighbor needed someone to reach out to. That's why He prompted me to put myself out there and say hi. God is the only one who can judge, but more importantly, He's the only one who can guide us to the people He needs us to reach out to so they can feel His love and unconditional acceptance, perhaps for the first time in their lives. And before you scoff at that notion…consider how you found me. I bet it wasn't just happenstance.

Over time I got to know this neighbor. I was surprised to discover he was driven and self-motivated just like me. He owned his own business and was very successful. He owned dirt bikes, four-wheelers, a home, and all this in his twenties. It was impressive.

Interestingly enough, not long after I introduced myself to this neighbor, he contracted hantavirus from cleaning out his garage. At the time, there was a concerning rash of new cases of hantavirus across the state, leaving everyone nervous, as its effects could be severe. My neighbor was one who became very ill and had to be hospitalized for several weeks.

By this time, Connie and I were aware our neighbor had no one. Imagine being ill to the point of hospitalization and not having a soul to depend on.

What if I hadn't followed that prompting?

We soon realized he would need someone to take care of his dog, a husky, who would require feeding and frequent walks. And Connie, being the thoughtful person she's always been, knew she would need to bring him some meals when he got home from the hospital. They were such small tasks for us, but for him, we could see it meant a lot.

There is something to be said about feeling needed, even in the smallest of ways. Knowing you were available, or aware, or equipped with just the right skill needed, at just the right moment to help another carries such a sense of peace and fulfillment. I fear few of us understand the hidden treasure trove of joy and wholeness that fills our hearts at that moment. And it only makes sense that we'd feel that way. If we're acting as God would have us do, isn't that akin to the feeling we feel when we do something worthy of making a respected mentor proud? Making God proud feels even more exhilarating.

Over the years, Connie and I have forged a relationship with that neighbor that is still meaningful and close to this day. He and I ended up having some surprising things in common and other things that were totally different, but our relationship wasn't about that. We didn't need to be on the same path. All it took was taking the time to know him. I had to let go of the urge to focus solely on my own personal pursuits, but my efforts were rewarded tenfold. That neighbor and I developed a relationship that will last for eternity merely because I chose to live in the present. And that cherished relationship was the reward I received for simply following a prompting.

This leads me to another key factor of living in the present and respecting another's journey—forgiveness. We cannot live and operate in the present while holding on to the past. That means grudges, old hurts, and self-loathing have to stop. Now. The only person you're hurting is you and the people who are trying to love you. The only person whose life you're oppressing is yours and those of the people you love. Honestly, most of the time, people you haven't forgiven don't even know you're angry at them. They're going about their lives free and easy while you're bound down by your feelings of hatred and vengeance concerning them.

Let. Go.

By allowing the grudge or hurt to continue, you give that person/people/event power. You're unwittingly giving them the power to control your life, and as a by-product, the lives of the people who love and care for you. Why perpetuate that power, that pain?

Stop.

Does it mean you have to figuratively or literally invite them over for tea or a backyard BBQ? Absolutely not. Forgiveness does not demand love and affection. It does not demand acceptance. In many ways, forgiveness is a gift to you, not to them. It means breaking the manacles and fetters of trauma and suffering, thereby allowing you to finally live free and in the present.

And if you need help with that, it's out there. There are all kinds of professionals available, ready and willing to help—especially if the person you need to forgive is yourself. If a professional isn't your bag at the moment, reach out to a buddy, a neighbor, or someone you trust.

Personally, I know there are all kinds of avenues and solutions for veterans. It's something that's near and dear to my heart. Veterans always have brothers and sisters willing to help fight any kind of foe, whether physical, mental, emotional, or spiritual.

Choosing to live in the present—to forgive, to let go, to focus on the moment—isn't always easy. In fact, most often it's one of the hardest things we can do. But I also know it's worth it. Try it. Test it yourself. The rewards for the effort are exponential.

Chapter 17

For the majority of our marriage, Connie and I have lived in the Utah Valley. It's comprised of many cities and towns and boasts two thriving universities. If you've ever lived in a university town, you know there is a constant flux of young people, and it's obvious when school is in session and when it's not. Often students will choose to live off-campus and find a condo or home to live in, so they can build a little equity during their college years rather than dumping money into rent.

In the late '80s and early '90s, we lived in a blue split-level home perched at the top of a slopping street in an average suburban neighborhood. One year, a group of rowdy, fun-loving university athletes moved into the house across from ours. They reminded me so much of the guy I had been at their age. Almost instantly, our family *adopted* that houseful of guys as if they were our own kids. They came over to our house for Sunday dinners, Connie helped them keep on top of their laundry, and they brought years of fun and laughter into our home.

Among that group of boys was a quarterback for Brigham Young University. Although he was a college football player, he and I had both loved baseball and basketball throughout our high school years. We found we had a lot in common and forged a friendship that has survived to this day.

It wasn't just the antics we got up to, though a particular night of launching bottle rockets and hiding under cars sticks out, or the time Connie sewed all the boys' socks and shirts shut. It was the feeling of family-even-without-being-family we felt. We looked out for each other and cared about each other with no strings attached.

One winter night, when Connie and I had driven several hours away to see her folks, we got snowed in and couldn't make it home. That night, the quarterback—who had recently won the prestigious Heisman Trophy (the highest honor in college football)—willingly trudged across the street in a raging blizzard to care for our small children despite the intense pressures and scrutiny he was under from the media.

As the years went by, we attended that young man's baptism and later his wedding. Even now decades later, we get together for a round of golf whenever he's in the area.

I owe that relationship to all that I've learned. My mentor taught me to love, to serve, and to live in the moment. And once I had a relationship with God, He taught me the same things, only more fully.

If you'll recall, "I love you" wasn't something we said in my home as a child. It took years and a patient mentor for me to see the power of showing love and saying the words. They hold such power, such influence. And it's amazing the devastation and razing effect that not showing and not saying has. A person who cannot say them will claim they're just words. To anyone denied those words, they're a weapon. Withholding them is a similitude of torture, especially to a spouse or child. Should words of love be bandied about? That's a harder question to answer. Does it water down the meaning or the intent? I don't know for certain, but my first thought is no. If there is anything the world is lacking today, it's love. The kind of love that is an action word, that's shown in word and deed. Imagine how our world would be different. No, it doesn't solve all the problems, but it sure makes them easier to bear.

Another word for love is *compassion*.

You may recall that I didn't see a doctor after I was struck by lightning. At the time, I felt fine, especially when I considered the devastating pain my friend Frank was in. What I didn't know, was that my brain function was irrevocably damaged. From the way it was explained to me by a neurologist, the connections in my brain couldn't be repaired; rather, my brain created new pathways, and sometimes those pathways didn't function as well as the old pathways did. As a result, I have headaches—migraines—that often result in stroke-like symptoms. Sometimes these effects leave me unable to speak and unable to walk.

Last year, I had such an episode, and it left me unable to walk for some time. When this happens, I often require medical and physical therapies that can take months to get me back on track.

Throughout my life, pain has been a fairly minor annoyance. I've been blessed with a skill that allows me to disassociate myself from any pain I feel, and the smallest doses of painkillers can leave me loopy. It wasn't until my latest brush with these recurring brain issues that I understood what severe pain is all about.

I'd been going through all kinds of therapies with little result. I had paralysis in both legs and was bound to a wheelchair. It was late at night. Connie had gone home, and the care facility I was in was dark and quiet. Like a bolt of lightning, pain suddenly shot down the nerves in one of my legs. The pain was excruciating, and every attempt I made to staunch the effects of disassociation did not work. After I paged the nurse, she ran into the room to find me writhing in pain. I remember praying to God in my mind. I recall begging Him, *Father, please, lead me, guide me, and walk beside me.* My prayer was answered as I was able to verbalize what I needed from the nurse. She pressed her knuckle deeply into my leg, raking over the nerve until the pain finally subsided.

I cannot express the relief and gratitude I felt toward that nurse—her compassion, her willingness to help, to listen, and to try. She rescued me in a hopeless, helpless moment. I realize the momentary pain I felt may seem like a small thing to some, but from my perspective, it was the worst physical pain I'd felt in my entire existence. For me, it wasn't a small thing.

I've always felt gratitude toward military personnel and first responders, but that day, their service was palpable, compassionate, and merciful. As a result of that experience, I better understood the sacrifices they make to bring relief, whether that relief is from fear, or pain, or suffering, or all the above. And the service they render can never fully be repaid. Words of thanks and meager paychecks are such a paltry offering.

Have you ever been in that situation before? It doesn't matter if the pain is psychological, physical, emotional, etc. When help arrives, there is no greater relief, even when actual relief from pain is not quite there yet. Just knowing they're there, that relief is imminent, makes all the difference.

But what if you have the kind of pain that isn't healed or helped with medicine, or bandages, or mental health professionals? If it's a pain in your soul, allow yourself to be helped. Try utilizing prayer. If you don't know how to pray, ask.

It may seem daunting, but prayer is simple. The gist is to first address God: "Dear God" or, "Heavenly Father". Second, thank Him for the blessings you do have in your life. Third, humbly and sincerely ask Him for what you need. Fourth, end your prayer with "in the name of Jesus Christ, amen."

Yes, it's that simple. The hard part is the faith and humility required to believe that He'll answer and send help. Also realize the help He sends isn't always what you want, but it's always, always what you need.

One of the important things I learned from my NDE is that angels are real.

The guide who came when I died and took me to the field I know was my guardian angel. He was someone I knew was there to help me. He was concerned for my welfare and was there to comfort and guide me through uncharted territory.

There were also people on the other side of the cloud, and I know they weren't random, unconcerned entities. They were part of my NDE, directly concerned with what was going on with me. I know there are people/angels who are continually concerned with our welfare and our progression when it comes to a life lived worthy of a good and joyous life's reliving. I'm convinced they're there in times of trial and in times of joy.

But there are earthly angels too, people living among you and me who selflessly care about those around them without care or need of compensation. It's my goal to be one of those people for others. I know it's a crucial component of a satisfactory life's reliving. How can I be a blessing to someone else? How can I relieve their pain and suffering? I've done my time in the military and I'm retired. And I'm still selfish. Selfish in that I get a rush and zing of joy when I'm able to help someone else, even in the smallest of ways. Neighbor in need of help with a garbage disposal? Zing. Man on the train in need of a few dollars to get by? Zing. A guy on the side of the road with a flat? Zing.

From my experience with angels, I know it's an honor to be one. We can't always be everything for everyone or heal all hurts, but we can certainly try and God will lead us to the ones who are praying for the smallest of miracles.

Try being an angel. It rocks.

Chapter 18

I wish I could explain death better. It's a topic I've had to engage in a lot lately. People seem desperate to know and understand death. They call, they message, they email. I find that I'm ill-equipped to verbalize everything I know on the subject. Because of that, every time I talk to people about death, I turn my part of the conversation over to God. It always amazes me that, by the end of the conversation, I'm nearly unaware of what I've said. Not that I'm complaining. I'd much rather the Holy Spirit explain death to a person who's wondering than just a regular guy like me. God knows what they need to hear. And again, I'm no prophet. I'm a simple guy who simply lets the promptings of the Spirit guide the conversation.

To try and answer the question, though, there is nothing to fear about death. Dying isn't painful. It's a process that's pure and done with love. Once outside your body, there is no pain. Instead, you're filled with peace.

When I was out of and above my body, I felt no pain—no pain in my hand, no aches from past sports injuries, not even hunger pains. And any worries were left behind. Every earthly care got replaced with a sense of wholeness, peace, unconditional love, and wonder at a new plane of existence. When it happens, most of what we think of as life's major challenges fade into insignificance. It doesn't matter what car you drove or how big your house was. It doesn't matter if you were famous or achieved society's highest honors. In fact, at your life's reliving, you find that everything you may have thought was worthy of praise carries no weight in the end. You're shocked to realize that it was in fact the little things that mattered: how you treated your loved ones, if you were thankful for what you were given, if you served your fellow men, if you loved unconditionally. In a way, we find our focus should have been trained in the opposite direction from what we're all told.

Maybe that's the easiest advice for me to give. What do you do to prepare for death? Pay attention to what high society does, expects, and says, then do exactly the opposite. All that stuff literally does not matter. You find that any time spent focused on society's expectations is an utter waste of the short time you have.

Imagine it. Do you think you'd ever be disappointed looking back at a life where the pure joy on another's face was what you lived for? Would you regret lifting another's burdens or enfolding a lost soul in unconditional acceptance? If you chose to live your life in such a way, I don't just think you'd be much happier, I know you would be, from personal experience.

Before you tell me it's easier said than done, I'll completely agree with you. It has taken death, being struck by lightning, and many other wake-up calls throughout my life to remind me where my focus should be. It's so easy to go with the flow of life as people tell us it should be. And that's just it. Change isn't easy. Being different isn't easy. Living a selfless life may not be easy or pay in worldly dividends, but the eternal blessings are beyond our comprehension and of far greater worth.

So where do you begin? You begin today, right now. Even if you start small. And always look forward. Move forward. Find a mentor, learn to forgive, appreciate the present, love and serve your neighbor, try your hand at prayer, and say and show love.

Have the faith and courage to test the idea. Go tell your spouse/child/family member that you love them, right now. If you aren't ready to serve a neighbor or stranger in need, then start with a smile or wave. But always pay attention to the result. Notice that you fill with light as you progress. Others will notice it too. Inexplicably, people will be happier around you; they'll want to be near you and wonder why you're suddenly so happy.

Then share what you've learned. Share a little of the light you've obtained with the next person, and the next. Watch how your new-found happiness can become contagious and spread. Of course, there will be those who balk and scoff. It's the nature of things. There must always be an opposite. But never let it discourage you.

May I also take a second and put in a plug for goals and becoming self-reliant? Free yourself from every form of bondage. Get out of debt, never put anything addictive into your body if you can help it, and reject unhealthy and controlling relationships. Freedom from bondage equals the opportunity to choose when, where, how, and why you do anything. And then as you enjoy more freedom, go and set good and worthy goals. Mark your progress, enjoy new possibilities, open the door to new ways to serve, and live a life of fulfillment.

Now concerning the death of loved ones, this element was a large part of why I decided to share my story after years of silence. Innumerable lives were affected by the devastation of the last few years. Few people escaped without the loss of someone dear.

Following my NDE, I had the privilege of experiencing funerals in a new way. Now when I attend a funeral service, I have an entirely different feeling. To me, it's a very calming feeling as I sit through the service. It's because I know that person—depending on what they went through in life—has been relieved of pain. Whatever they went through here on this earth, they don't have to go through that pain anymore. No leg, back, head, joint, heart, or mental discomfort or pain ever again. That pain is lifted from their body the moment they're released from this earthly world. It's instant. It's gone. Therefore, there is no need to mourn for them. Yes, miss them, but don't mourn for them. Imagine the joy of returning to full health and a whole mind and body! What a sweet gift.

Missing them is natural and expected. But here's another thing I learned after my NDE: we will see them again, and they are with us even though we may not see them. Remember those people on the other side of the cloud? They are our loved ones. They are at peace and simply await the day when it's our turn to return home. I felt them there. Their love and support was palpable. We will see them again.

Until you see them again, live your best life. Make them proud. Show them you now know the secret to receiving a good reliving of life. What greater gift can you give them than to make it back to them having lived a life of selflessness and joy?

My life before this was fraught with selfishness, greed, and a relentless drive for success in business. What I learned most from my NDE is to not look back. Don't look back at what you've done in your life. Take a good look at your life as it is today, right now. And start looking toward the future. We can change if we want to. If you want to make a difference, just be kind to somebody—be kind to a friend, a fellow worker, or a neighbor. Discover the reaction you get by being kind to them. Most people are very defensive, but there's something about love that calms people down. This life isn't about how much we make. It isn't about prestige or power. It's about *the One*. It's about each life we can affect for good.

At this stage in my life, I enjoy eating dessert first. I enjoy planting flowers to remind me of my time in the field. I strive to live every day just a little better than the one before and to keep moving forward. I grab every opportunity to serve my fellow men. Family, love, and God fill my life with the joy I strive to deserve.

There are some scripture verses that I'd like to share with you. They pretty well sum up how to prepare for the future:

> But behold, all things have been done in the wisdom of him who knoweth all things.
>
> Adam fell that men might be; and men are, that they might have joy.
>
> And the Messiah cometh in the fulness of time, that he may redeem the children of men from the fall. And because that they are redeemed from the fall they have become free forever, knowing good from evil; to act for themselves and not to be acted upon, save it be by the punishment of the law at the great and last day, according to the commandments which God hath given.
>
> Wherefore, men are free according to the flesh; and all things are given them which are expedient unto man. And they are free to

choose liberty and eternal life, through the great
Mediator of all men, or to choose captivity and
death, according to the captivity and power of
the devil; for he seeketh that all men might be
miserable like unto himself.

This earthly life was created by a loving God who knows everything. We were sent here to learn how to live good and joy-filled lives
of service to our loved ones, friends, and fellow men. Jesus Christ is
real and atoned for our mistakes so that we can be free. His sacrifice made it possible for us to choose how our life will turn out. We
have everything we need. Now we must choose to live a life like the
Savior's: compassionate, selfless, fulfilling.

I want to share my testimony (my sure beliefs) with you, that
God loves you, and He wants all His children to find their way back
home. I believe that starting today. We can be kind to others—be a
true friend. Be sincere and listen to others' needs. Pray to God. Thank
Him for your blessings. Then ask Him for help. He will answer you.

In the name of Jesus Christ, amen.

Acknowledgments

T o my wife, Connie, without her patience, love, understanding, and personal sacrifice, it would not have all been possible. Thank you for keeping me grounded and enjoying life with me. You are my best friend.

To Martin Tanner, thank you for all the advice but most of all your friendship and patience.

Thanks to my neighbor and friend, Wes Lapioli. You were inspired to ask me for an interview. The YouTube video has many views from around the world. What a humbling experience this has been (prioritizeyourlife.com).

Thanks to Frank Purvis for your input and for being a true friend for the past forty-plus years.

To Lilia Samoilo, thank you for being my eternal friend and giving me direction and NDE counseling. Thanks for your support for combat soldiers and veterans (NDE Radio).

Last but not least, to Sandy Ponton, my ghostwriter. What a joy it has been to work on this project with you. Thanks to your family for their patience and time on my behalf. Your writing has truly been inspired.

About the Author

Drafted to the Vietnam War at the tender age of eighteen, Scott played all-army basketball and eventually earned a coveted spot as a professional baller for a German club.

While stationed in Germany, he married his sweetheart, Connie Warner Drummond. Their nearly fifty years of marriage has blessed them with four children, twelve grandchildren, and joyous memories that will last an eternity.

Upon his release from the army, Scott played baseball for Brigham Young University. While he attended classes there, the United States Postal Service hired him with an offer he couldn't refuse. After thirty years, Scott retired as a respected postmaster.

Scott's interests include sports, vegetable and flower gardening, and traveling as often as possible with Connie.

One of the highlights of Scott and Connie's life together was serving two missions for the Church of Jesus Christ of Latter-Day Saints. The memories and lives they touched will remain in their hearts forever.

Because Scott knows that life should be relished, one of his little indulgences is eating pie before his dinner.

Gracie Scott Foundation

June 2012 brought an angel into the lives of Scott and Connie Drummond. This blessed event was the premature birth of their precious granddaughter Gracie. The joy she brings into their lives inspired them to form the Gracie Scott Foundation whose mission is to change the lives of children with special needs for the better.

Portions of the proceeds from this book will be donated to the Gracie Scott Foundation whose purpose is to provide funds for special-needs children to attend camps and change their lives for the better.

For more information, please visit graciescott.org

Thank you.